HOW TO BECOME

THE KEY LEADER

THE NEW TRAITS AND HOW TO USE THEM TO DRIVE REAL GROWTH

By Ali Kursun

First published by sparkChief & Co. in 2019

Note to Librarians: A cataloguing record for this book is available from Swiss National Library (NL) in Switzerland at http://www.helveticat.ch

ISBN 9781791869250

sparkChief Publishing

This book was published on-demand in cooperation with sparkChief & Co. Publishing. On-demand publishing is a unique process and service of making a book available for retail sale to the public taking advantage of on-demand manufacturing and internet marketing. On-demand publishing includes promotions, retail sales, manufacturing, order fulfilment, accounting and collecting royalties on behalf of the author.

For international book sales:

sparkChief & Co. Publishing

25 Route de Lullier

1254 Jussy, Geneva, SWITZERLAND

phone +41 22 346 24 05; email to bookorders@sparkchief.com

Order online at:

www.sparkchief.com/services_book.html

Also available on amazon.com and other online book sellers.

To the future of brave leaders who desperately are
needed to maximise value for all stakeholders

TABLE OF CONTENTS

ACKNOWLEDGEMENT

My thanks are due to many clients and various people.

I wish to thank those who directly supported me with the thinking described here and, especially Virginia (Ginny) McMorrow, my amazing long-time friend and editor, who was again so instrumental in the way she directed me and helped me to develop this new manuscript.

Many clients, colleagues, and partners contributed to this book over the last couple of years. Finally, my thanks to all who have invited me to speak to them and who remind me that this work really does make a difference.

Many thanks to you all!

INTRODUCTION:

Why Invest in Leaders as Formula 1 Drivers?

Investors/shareholders should view the leadership of the companies in which they invest as Formula One drivers. In Formula One racing, all cars are state of the art. The same is true of many top companies (though, sadly, not all), thanks to their management systems and proactive strategies. In addition to the unparalleled teamwork and cooperation illustrated by the racing crew/leadership, the difference in winning the race/viability is, ultimately, the driver/leader. The best driver(leader) provides the opportunity and possibility to win big time (achieve sustainability, financial viability, and stakeholder value).

But with the wrong driver/leader, although you are still in the race/market and possess a good image/return on capital invested, you are "under-utilising" the powerful engine of your car/company and capital invested. Unfortunately, that under-performing scenario is present in many well-established companies today that are not successful in achieving their optimal potential.

So, what should you do? The practical and common sense answer is twofold:

1. Invest in technology, tools, systems, and approaches to help you identify, engage, and retain "only" the right leaders who can drive your company in the most efficient and effective

manner possible toward the mile markers and ultimate finish line.

2. Stop arbitrarily picking people. Instead, start knowing who can truly drive your business at all levels – organisation, division, function, group, and team – if you want to outperform and succeed long-term with a company that balances the needs of all stakeholders as far as practically possible.

In other words, hire a talented driver, rev the powerful engines, and go!

SECTION 1:

LEADERSHIP TRAITS

Self-Identifying as a Leader

CHAPTER 1

Are You a Don't Rock the Boat Leader or Leader Who Rocks?

Leaders come in different formats, sizes, and designs – with their own experience, skill, and personal style. Although there is undeniable personal bias in a leadership style, there is also as much undeniable influence of context in how that specific leader behaves in a given leadership role. Throughout my consulting engagements over many years, I have met four types of leaders who are quite distinct in the way they conduct business, lead their organisations, and manage people.

The key question regarding leadership involves assessing and knowing what you should expect in the individual's capacity and ability to lead change when required. There is no doubt that today's leaders need to breathe change to survive and add value to whatever mandate and organisational goals they are expected to achieve. At the very least, we all need to acknowledge that today's leaders face enormous responsibility, accountability, and pressure to perform as no leadership role is easy to conduct. Although we need to respect the efforts and ambitions of leaders who give their best to do a good job given their context, we also need to be crystal clear on what we expect from such an individual in terms of anticipated results in a given environment.

The following four leadership definitions may help management to understand what they should expect from a leader's performance in a given organisational context.

4 TYPES OF LEADERS

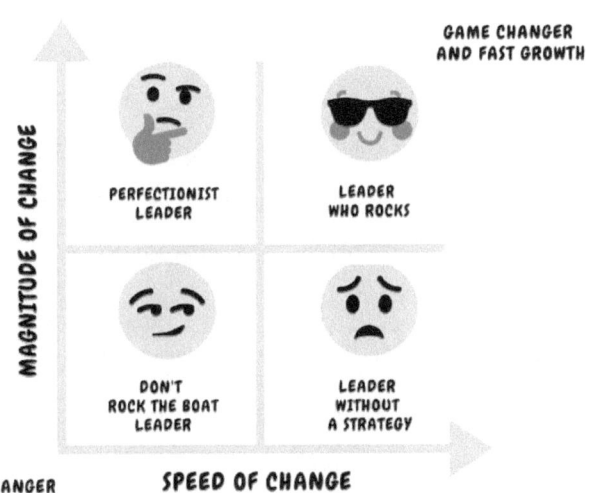

Source: sparkChief & Co.

1. Don't Rock the Boat Leader

This leader type has become the most popular in many companies for a number of reasons, primarily because such individuals provide acceptable stable growth and deliver results according to agreed-upon plans and budgets. However, you cannot expect this leader type to drastically drive significant transformation or innovative initiatives or exceed objectives because it is simply not designed to do so. No surprises or high expectations are requirements of the person who fulfils this type of role. Instead, acceptable and consistent results will do as long as the company's stock value moves slowly and steadily upwards year after year. If you want steady and satisfactory revenues and profits, these are the leaders whom you want to operate and manage your business.

Think of them as treasury bonds. They deliver acceptable returns from a safe and stable operation year after year. It is a perfect leadership type, especially if you have a "cash cow" business. After all, why even think about changing the cow if it provides milk day after day?

2. Perfectionist Leader

These leaders are strategic but move slowly because they usually want, for example, to launch the perfect product or service with the perfect design and perfect market conditions. Or, they consider all the innumerable potential probabilities of impact on a transformation initiative that could change the direction of the organisation. They may have difficulties synthesising the information presented and cannot make up their minds easily. Often taking too much time to decide and implement any change initiative, they run the risk of staying behind the curve. Although they are survivors, they are becoming less and less popular due to ever-increasing competitive market conditions.

Think of them as novelists who edit and revise their draft manuscripts over and over, refusing to let them go and submit them to publishers until all words and grammatical references are perfect. By the time they are ready to send their masterpieces off into the world, the editors and/or readers are no longer interested in what they have to say.

3. Leader Without a Strategy

The main concern of this leader type is driving change regardless of the impact on the organisation, its overall strategy, its goals, and its vision. Mostly swamped with many small change projects, such leaders often feel overwhelmed with the amount of effort required to bring projects to a successful end. This leader type excels in putting out fires and responding to short-term crises, typically following the latest market trends without significant research into whether the new strategy suits the company. Desiring to look progressive and proactive, they succeed in looking busy. Yet, stakeholders may wonder what results they actually achieve in light of the expenditure of time, money, and resources.

Think of such a leader as a busy bee, buzzing around, delegating tasks, but without a central focus. Things may be accomplished, but the impact on the whole organisation may not be optimal or desirable.

4. Leader Who Rocks

Leaders who rock have the ability to drive major transformational change and innovative initiatives and lead others – not with their assumed authority, but because of their convincing vision and highly compelling ideas and insights about the business. They are not afraid of failure and are willing to take highly complex, yet calculated, risks. At the forefront of not only fact-based but truth-based decision making, such leaders are great listeners, as well as experts on knowing to whom they should listen. They spread wisdom and are champions of knowledge sharing. Possessing the ability and capacity to view the future so vividly, leaders who rock persuade others around them to become true believers who come to see and are willing to share the same future.

Leaders who rock move fast, relentlessly, with accurate information on hand, and with super focus on the best outcome for all stakeholders. They do not differentiate among stakeholders; they are purely interested in building the best, most profitable, and sustainable businesses for the future.

Think of them as charismatic rock stars who have true talent and the ability to have an effect on their audience – who can lift their fans higher with a positive message and subtly impact their lives.

Make Sure You Select the Right Leader to Grow your Business

The bottom line is this: Acknowledging and understanding the type of leaders you hire, develop, and retain to operate and grow your business is mission critical to its future success. There is no point of putting "don't rock the boat leaders" in roles where you expect them to significantly transform and grow your business. At the other extreme, placing a "leader who rocks" into a position where you only want consistent, acceptable, and stable growth is not an optimal use of talent either. Perfectionists and no-strategy leaders fall somewhere in between and work best only in environments that value slow growth or short-term planning.

With the appropriate, practical, and truthful optics — in terms of future growth plans and expectations — management can compose a more realistically aligned leadership team to drive stakeholder value, productivity, and efficiency according to realistic organisation capacity and capability. In the end, all stakeholders – leaders, employees, shareholders, and the community at large – stand to benefit from forward-looking, proactive, and intelligent decisions that may significantly affect all parties.

LEADERSHIP TRAITS

On the Job

CHAPTER 2

5 Needs Every Leader Should Embrace; Building Blocks for Optimal Leadership

Every person is, or should be, his or her own leader — whether a student, educator, employee, business executive, or government official. Understanding that one should not seek leadership in others, but in oneself, is the starting point to truly strive toward having a better family, community, society, organisation, corporation, and nation.

As a leader, to be and do one's best, to outperform, requires clear and informed thought processes and actions. With this foundation, leaders can minimise unnecessary and damaging costs to themselves, as well as the individuals and organisations for which they share responsibility.

1. The Need for Transparency

There has been a movement toward transparency since the beginning of the technological advancement in every field. In my point of view, this movement represents the biggest revolution of all. Although technology will continue to bring more openness and transparency in our lives, communities, societies, corporations, and nations, the result may not be something that everyone desires. But we need to empower transparency for ourselves and as a member of society. If we are genuinely honest with ourselves, we can reach our own truths faster.

In the end, transparency will serve all stakeholders, including organisations as a whole; the more they become transparent, the better and more effectively they will serve their shareholders, customers, and workforce. Unfortunately, all stakeholders do not empower, or believe in, this movement, with the opposite true in many organisations. For example, shareholders are not transparent with management, management is not transparent with employees, and employees are not transparent with management – yet alone with themselves. This non-transparency triggers huge hidden costs from wasted resources, finances, and time for all stakeholders – expenditures that many leadership teams might not be able to evaluate or recognise. But hidden or not, this cost in one that all of society continues to pay.

2. The Need to Uncover Potential: Unemployed vs. Untapped

The term that defines the population who do not hold a job – "unemployed" – is very misguided, most likely coined originally by people with an archaic vision of modern economy and society (and, perhaps, explain why there has not been a newer version). As defined in Investopedia.com, "unemployment is a phenomenon that occurs when a person who is actively searching for employment is unable to find work. Unemployment is often used as a measure of the health of the economy. The most frequently measure of unemployment is the unemployment rate, which is the number of unemployed people divided by the number of people in the labour force."

This explanation is, by far, the least insightful definition of unemployment, solely based on a single-minded and irresponsible view of the condition. The majority of people who fall into this category are totally capable individuals with their own convictions, passions, values, and meanings of life. It is just that the organisations (people) that employed them earlier did not know how to extract, or were not at all interested in extracting, the potential of these individuals.

The true term should be "untapped" rather than "unemployed" people. Organisations (people) that are unable or incompetent to tap into the potential of their workforce should be fined (or, perhaps, taxed) or left unemployed until they learn otherwise. If not, we will continue to pay the cost for the very few who either remain ignorant or purposefully exploit society at large.

3. The Need to Choose

Margaret Lobenstine's book, The Renaissance Soul: Life Design for People with Too Many Passions to Pick Just One, deals with the dilemma of wanting to follow multiple passions rather than confining oneself to only one. She contemplates that the people with this characteristic have "Renaissance Souls," which is a more positive attribute of people who might consider themselves to be confused. Wanting to do many things or be as many persons as one might desire is not a problem. It just might require much more energy, ambition, and will power.

With the majority of people struggling to just find a single passion, I think her real message is that you do not need to limit yourself with one interest. But in the end, you still need to choose and focus on the area in which you shine most brightly. If your passions are multiple, stick with them. But make a choice so you do not go through the rest of your life wondering if you took the right path.

4. The Need to Ask the Right Questions

Being able to focus on whatever you do is probably one of the most critical, but underestimated and undervalued, aptitudes in many people's lives. It is not an easy skill to possess, as it requires discipline and practice. To paint a complete picture of ourselves, we must focus on the right things – be it at a personal or organisational level – by asking the right questions. The wrong questions will only waste time as you attempt to find the irrelevant answers to your challenges, which is one reason why some people or businesses struggle with their core.

Asking the right questions requires deep contextual understanding of what is it that you are trying to do – again, whether at the personal or organisational level – which may be why many organisations (people) are frequently tempted to answer only familiar questions. For example, when companies face what I call the "efficiency disease" – a chronic inflammatory condition caused by forced price competition, while constantly trying to find savings without the deep insights of the overall well-being of the organisation and all its stakeholders – they tend to focus on the easiest way out: cutting tangible costs. This short-term solution can, and often does, result in a much deeper pain afterwards.

As Dr. John McDougal states in his website, drmcdougall.com, "people love to hear good news about their bad habits." They easily postpone unfelt pain through quick fixes of relief today, not caring about their future state. When challenged by potential future conditions, they dismiss compassion for the love of today's pleasure. It is this inability that needs to be developed and progressed, so we can improve the condition and well-being of individuals, families, communities, organisations, nations, and the environment.

5. The Need to Act

The joke about the person who hopes to win the lotto without actually playing a game has the expected moral of the story: You need to act if you want something to happen. I have met people in all corners of the world and organisations who share the same thought as in the joke, passing the expectation of action to someone else. They say they are not accountable for taking action, which requires energy and compassion, at the very least, for oneself.

But without action, one's life may not move forward. To begin, the first ingredient for action is compassion. To have compassion for oneself (and others, if you are a bit more progressive), you need to prepare the groundwork, which begins within the family. If you are fortunate enough to have compassion very early in life, thanks to your family environment, taking action might be much easier. However, not all of us are lucky, growing up in very diverse family scenarios, which delays our capacity for compassion. We also cannot expect everyone to be compassionate; if that were true, our world would be a much different and more advanced place.

The need to act to change things for the better and improve the lives of millions who are stuck in ignorance, or transform the minds of people who purposefully force others to remain in ignorance, is probably the most important mission we all must embark on. That need starts with each and every one of us.

One Final Word

Leadership – on a personal and organisational level – requires clarity, compassion, knowledge, confidence, humility, courage, and a host of other critical traits. Today's complex and chaotic world requires – or, rather, demands – genuine leaders in order to transform problems into solutions, and questions into answers. Together, sound thinking and action can create a ripple effect to enhance the well-being of every person they touch.

CHAPTER 3

5 Career Mistakes Every Leader Should Avoid

No matter their experience level and knowledge, at some point in their work life, most leaders make one or more mistakes that have the potential to derail or stall their career path. Understanding the fallacy inherent in these mistakes, or beliefs, is crucial to positioning oneself to be offered and to accept growth opportunities that can satisfy the goals and desires of both the organisation and the individual.

Mistake 1. Even though the definition of "success" is not clearly defined or communicated in your organisation, you still expect to be fairly promoted.

Success means different things to different people. Consequently, it is extremely important to view the definition under a reality microscope. For example, some businesses define success as 3% to 5% growth per year, while others cite 10% to 15% or even 20%+. Accelerated career opportunities happen mostly in fast-growing business environments. That said, since the growth rate is a key indicator of career progression in any organisation, there is no point in expecting fast movement if your business is in a slow-growth industry.

Exacerbating the situation, some businesses do not provide transparency on what success means in terms of leadership career progression, as well as the company's financial viability. Without clear communication of the goals to which one should aspire, the chance to discover and take advantage of growth opportunities becomes exceedingly difficult.

Mistake 2. You are not close to the centre of the "success" party, but you still think you are a key participant.

Watch carefully who are the hosts at the centre of the success party in your organisation – and observe your distance from the centre of the party. If you are at the periphery, you are simply a guest.

Rather than waiting for an invitation to each party, leaders should take responsibility in determining how to transform their roles from guest to host. Discover the rules of the game, make the right connections within successful networks, take the steps to move from the periphery and ever closer toward the centre, and organise your own parties.

And in any situation, guests come and go, while hosts remain the same. If you cannot be a host in your organisation, and desire real growth opportunities, then you need to find another home.

Mistake 3. Although the same players are passed the ball all the time, you are still waiting for someone to pass the ball to you.

Picture this scenario: You think that you are as talented as others in the organisation. In fact, you attend the same training sessions, participate in the same meetings, contribute the same way and as much as others do, and present yourself as part of the same leadership team. But when it comes to new career opportunities and initiatives, no one is talking to you. In fact, no one even mentions your name.

Most of the time, management passes the "opportunity ball" to the same players in the team. Nobody gives you the opportunity to grow a business or drive a strategic project that is critical to the success of your organisation. You never get to touch the "opportunity ball" or even approach it. In fact, you are simply a spectator. Actual players and spectators enjoy the game in very different ways. Don't ever make the mistake in assuming that because you are part of a team, you will eventually get to play.

Mistake 4. Others silently stop supporting you, but you still believe that receiving no feedback is a good thing.

The most important point to recognise in your career is the precise moment when others "silently" stop supporting you. Failing to acknowledge this point, because of any reason – such as having a stable position, a slow but consistent salary progression, or a happy office environment – will trick your mind falsely and hamper your career.

You need to be serious, conscious, and realistic at all times on how others communicate with you and provide feedback – particularly if there is no feedback. If others silently stop supporting you, understand that it means they will not stand up for you when you need help. In truth, they may abandon you to your own devices when you are in most need of support or assistance – resulting in you getting stuck in avoidable situations. After all, successful leaders go nowhere without the support of other people.

Mistake 5. You are not developing your career like an entrepreneur, yet you still believe that someone will develop it for you.

You are not learning or doing anything to continuously improve your knowledge, expertise, and exposure to networks outside your organisation. In addition, you naively believe that just being employed actually increases your level of employability.

Don't accept mediocrity. Whatever you decide to learn, go deep so that you are able to bring fresh insights to others and receive recognition not only within your organisation – but most importantly, outside of it. After all, you may decide to leave the company, or perhaps your employer decides to let you go. In either case, remember that your personal brand needs to be much better than your employer's brand. Although conventional wisdom dictates the opposite – that is, if you work for a good brand, it should be easier to find another position – it is absolutely not true in today's context. As jobs become more and more scarce, the importance of impactful individual contribution increases exponentially.

Others outside your organisation need to first recognise your brand, then your employer's brand. In fact, you are part of your current employer's brand. That said, if you are currently working for a good organisation, management already acknowledges that truth because they could not build a good brand without treating you as an essential component of their brand.

Take Responsibility for Your Mistakes

The bottom line is simply as follows: It is inevitable that leaders will make one or more mistakes in advancing up their career ladder. But these errors in judgment are avoidable – or, at least, repairable – if one understands why such thinking doesn't work. Leaders must take responsibility for understanding what success means to their career growth and then go after it. To achieve desired goals, leaders should consider themselves as entrepreneurs, even within the confines of an employer's organisation.

Never, ever stop learning to renew yourself to become a key player. The future is so bright for those who deeply understand how important it is to believe a simple truth: It is never too late to discover new opportunities, and the only person who should care about you is you.

CHAPTER 4

5 Things Not to Say in a Leadership Role

People don't need to be led. They'd rather have the opportunity to follow a natural leader (a guide) so that they also learn how to lead themselves and others in any given environment – be it career-related or personal. Therefore, people in leadership roles have a tremendous responsibility to speak the truth and not just "shoot from the hip." Leaders must understand, and consider with care, the meaning of each word they utter, as well as act as role models to encourage others' future growth and organisational continuity.

In light of so many buzz words used today, it is important to pause and question some of the common sayings that leaders might use – without considering the implications – when they perform in a leadership capacity. To be truthful to themselves, as well as to others who fall under their responsibility, leaders should avoid the following five common statements.

Statement 1. We are a family. This overused term makes the claim to others that they are part of a family. If leaders in your organisation walk around and tell employees that they are part of a family, remember this key point: "Parents do not fire their children when things don't work for them!" Business is business. There is no need to make promises you cannot keep – or misuse a sentiment that is false and misleading.

Statement 2. I am authentic. Being authentic is a luxury few people can afford in a business environment. Obviously, if you are in a leadership role, possessing power and authority, you might entertain the idea of being authentic. However, be cautious about telling others to be authentic as well. Authenticity requires an enormous amount of transparency. That said, don't say "I am authentic" and encourage others to be so if you are not 100% sure your organisational culture actually encourages and supports authenticity, instead of mouthing nice-sounding phrases. Since a picture is often worth 1,000 words, the cartoon below clearly illustrates what it means to be "authentic" without power to support oneself.

Statement 3. I am looking forward to this new adventure or challenge. People who take on new leadership roles are the most likely individuals to make this comment. Please don't say these words! If you want a new adventure and challenge, embark on a hiking expedition or exotic trip in the wild. A person looking up to you as a leader needs to see someone who is not only "super confident" about the upcoming role as a leader for the business, but also radiates confidence to support the employee as an individual and team member. Consider how you would feel, boarding a plane and hearing the pilot say that he or she is looking forward to this new trip as an adventure or a challenge. I'd shout, "Please get me off this plane right now!" Anyone would prefer to board another plane where the pilot is poised and self-possessed at the idea of going from point A to point B (and making sure you arrive safely).

A word of advice to new leaders who want to say something meaningful to their staff: Simply state that you are honored to be given the leadership role and that you take it – and the responsibility that accompanies the position – seriously.

Statement 4. We should all embrace change. If you have ever been involved in a change management project or initiative, you should realise by now that people equate change to something new, and new equates to something "unproven" – which makes it a double unknown. This fact underlies why so many change management projects fail to achieve their expected outcomes.

Consider: When you know that change will bring some unknowns to people's lives, why should you tell them to embrace it? Human nature has proven again and again that people will resist change when they do not know what that change will mean for their circumstances. By saying these words (about embracing change) and knowing what they really mean, you are, in reality, telling others that you know about "something" but cannot tell them what it means for them! If you know about something (whatever that may be) that will change the way people work or put them out of work, it is better to provide hints rather than hiding things until the change knocks on the door. This approach of honest communication is much more efficient than telling employees nonsense and wasting time for the organisation and the people whom you expect to believe what you say.

Statement 5. And let's not forget to have some fun. Having fun at work is a great thing if everyone is on the same page and enjoying it. However, if you have no clue as to whether people enjoy their current roles, what they think about their organisation culture, and how they view their relationship with their leaders — and then tell them to have "fun" — you might be implying that they should celebrate these unknowns. Before making such a suggestion, make sure that people in your organisation truly enjoy what they are doing, feel comfortable being who they are and want to be, and embrace their current leadership.

Here is the bottom line: Leadership roles are not meant for managers to persuade others to believe that they are part of a family, to encourage them to have an adventure, to tell others to be themselves when they are clueless as to how competitive and frustrating it is out there for others, to embrace change, or to inspire them to have fun and "whistle while they work." Leadership roles are serious business, not for children or immature people who cannot even lead themselves. Leadership roles are not about you but about others. Leadership roles are for people who genuinely want to help others succeed.

CHAPTER 5

5 Leadership Misconceptions That Are Bad for Business

We live in a world of contradictions and very easily lose focus on what is most important. When it comes to business, the most essential goal on which all participants in any enterprise should focus is to maximise returns for all stakeholders. Everything else is auxiliary and should support this main objective.

Consider this point from just a sampling of stakeholder perspectives, of which the list is endless:

- As shareholders, we want to invest in companies that provide us with the highest return.
- As employees, we want to work for companies that provide us with the maximum value for the contributions we make.
- As clients, we want to buy products and services from companies that provide us with the maximum value for which we pay.
- As suppliers, we want to work with companies that provide us with maximum growth opportunities for our business.

In light of this most crucial understanding of business, it makes very little sense to deceive any stakeholder, either in the short- or long-term. If any party feels deceived or misled, the after-effect of that deception will hurt all other stakeholders at some point in ways that are not necessarily easily observable or straight forward.

Walking the Talk Leads to Accountability

Consequently, true business leaders need to consider themselves as the "champions of value optimisation" for all stakeholders. Employees (contrary to what the employees themselves may think) are important stakeholders and, therefore, not exempt from this process or effort. There is no point in "saying something" but "doing something else" when it comes to managing a business. Believe it or not, every stakeholder pays attention (or should) to leadership's "walking the talk."

The following five common (often unintentional) leadership misconceptions can have an adverse impact on an organisation's performance. Some leaders may not even realise that they are thinking in certain ways. Consequently, it is crucial for them to recognise such thought patterns as they occur and discourage others from those same thought patterns.

Misconception 1. Asking Leaders to Set Their Feelings Aside

Decisions we make about people are all personal. There is no need to deny the opposite. Organisations that encourage impersonal people decisions miss a very critical point about conducting a successful and viable business. To be successful, an organisation needs people who are equipped with both logic and deep human-sensing capability. If you tell your people to set their feeling aside or stop feeling compassion for others, they will lose their ability to empathise with colleagues – and, ultimately, anyone with whom they interact in their day-to-day encounters. When people become desensitised, it becomes more difficult for them to make sense out of anything and to see things clearly.

Companies need people with more common sense – and empathy – to improve situations at whatever level they occur in the organisation. Hiring passionate and compassionate people or telling your employees to possess those capabilities, while asking them to put their feelings aside with regard to people decisions, does not make any sense. In fact, it can only damage leadership when stakeholders then view the leadership team as communicating mixed signals.

Misconception 2. Believing Social Responsibility Is an External Act

Before you jump into supporting the community at large and fulfill your social responsibility as an organisation, you must first ensure that you have taken care of your own people. Advocating social responsibility in the public eye but then neglecting the true development of your own employees is not social responsibility. In fact, it is comparable to acting in a hypocritical or indifferent manner, with stakeholders perceiving leadership to be more concerned with their public image.

Leaders need to ensure that every member of the employee population has developed a sense of belonging to the organisation's cause and mission, is able to develop and grow as individuals, feels fairly rewarded, engages fully, and is willing to creatively contribute and generate value not only for one's self but also for the corporate population to which the individual belongs. Only then is the organisation ready to fulfil its duty of social responsibility at large. Actually, when you are fully taking care of your own employees, you are truly in the process of fulling your social responsibility within the communities where those employees live and work.

Misconception 3. Focusing Only on Short-Term Cost Measures

Efficient and productive business operations should be a top priority for any business. However, asking employees to be cost conscious, efficient, and productive, but then wasting valuable resources by hiring, developing, and retaining the "wrong" people to manage the business, is not a practical or efficient practice. This behaviour is comparable to running a business with a hole in your pocket. What is the point of asking people to save money when you have a gaping hole in your pocket? You need to sew that pocket shut gradually, a process that starts with hiring "only" the right people to grow your business.

But more than that, short-term cost efficiency is meaningless in the long-term if it does not resolve the company's wasteful endeavours. Consideration of both the near and distant future should accompany every financial decision.

Misconception 4. Assuming Talent Has an Age (or, Expiration Date)

Many companies complain about the lack of qualified candidates in today's highly competitive market. Yet, they totally ignore, downplay, or refuse to consider proactive strategies that will enable them to retain the most experienced, skilled, and potentially "least costly" employee segment in the organisation: AKA, seniors.

If you truly understand what "talent" means, you recognise that talent has no age, gender, ethnicity, or any other classification. Many talent management programmes, in fact, do not even include the senior employee population as if "talent" per se has an age! Using the vast experience and skill levels of this group – and enhancing these skills to meet a company's future needs – allows the organisation to retain a knowledgeable perspective on where the company has been and where it is going. This perspective, when shared with younger employees, can help lower the costs of hiring the wrong individuals, while empowering all age groups as positive contributors to the company's growth.

Misconception 5. Thinking Innovation Is Just a Corporate Programme

Truly innovative organisations actually do not have any so-called innovation programmes, because they strongly believe that innovation should be an organic process throughout the enterprise. Such an organic approach literally means that all individuals are expected to be inventive and resourceful in their own ways and with regard to their job responsibilities. But that approach also requires a very different organisational culture than that found in companies that view innovation as just another corporate programme, one that expects creative outcomes from only a select number of designated employees.

Organisations that practice and encourage true innovation are comfortable with the creative process and know that its essence is to develop something new and valuable. They also recognise that innovation involves risk, that their organisational culture will not punish employees who fail during the process, and that punishing failure blocks innovation. After all, punishing people when they fail guarantees they will never try again.

Clear Vision Leads to Successful Growth

The bottom line is simple: We cannot build and grow sustainable businesses based on misconceived perspectives. There was a time when what one said and what one did was not easily verifiable, either because nobody dared to challenge the status quo or lacked the technology/tools to validate such claims. This scenario is no longer true. Today, we have the technological capability and new approaches to make things clearer and more accountable for all stakeholders.

In addition, more and more employees, as part of an essential requirement of committing to a specific organisation in a true partnership, want more transparency and integrity. Luckily! Talented employees do not want to be played with, do not want to waste time, and do not wish to be deceived. They seek genuine accountability in leadership. In other words, they want their leaders to walk the talk.

If we want to align our organisations with a more promising future, the time is now to start matching our actions to our words. In essence, we all need to walk the talk in order to design and develop better performing organisations for the future.

CHAPTER 6

Why Strategy Works to Address Misperceptions of Career Growth

Based on hundreds of appraisals and interviews with individuals of diverse gender, age, or education – while assessing their personal development (mostly career-related, but also dealing with life and self-fulfilment) – I have observed the most common problem to arise dealt with strategy (or, lack of it). In other words, many people fail to construct strategies to achieve a more fulfilling future. In fact, many people lack guidelines or frameworks that would enable them to develop effective strategies for their careers, lives, or relationships.

This observation is not as surprising as one might think, since a significant majority of people, in general, never receive formal guidelines as to how to live their lives satisfactorily or progress in their careers. Consider parenthood. Despite having numerous resources to draw upon when having a child, no parent goes to an institutional "school for parenthood"— although this topic could potentially be a university degree!

The same lack of formal preparedness too often occurs with regard to decisions about what one should do in life or how to move up the job hierarchy. Typical (and practical) human behaviour leads an individual to find a job after graduation. After that, you are expected to navigate on your own to determine how to move forward, usually without a framework to help navigate the stormy weathers of your career. On the way, if you are "lucky," some people will offer their own success stories, which will prompt you to try and live those stories yourself. But that is where the flaw lies, along with the misperceptions such stories engender.

The Better Choice to Avoid Misperceptions

While success stories are encouraging, one must remember what they truly are – just stories – and not effective strategies. These positive tales are more about heroism and how one dealt with a specific situation, overcame a difficulty, and so on. Strategies, on the other hand, involve a framework, which will serve as a practical tool and guideline for dealing with any situation.

Consider this old concept: If you want to help poor people, don't give them money. Instead, teach them how to fish, thereby providing a more sustainable solution to poverty. In this analogy, "a story" would be the money, and the "framework" would be "teaching how to fish." Some people relate to an eager audience how they followed their passion, which explains their success. Or, perhaps, they became experts on a subject by studying and working 10,000 hours on it! These are all anecdotes, not frameworks – and to be successful, everyone needs some type of framework.

Too often, as a result of these narratives, people face a number of misperceptions that are driven by "observed realities." It is critical for anyone who is currently planning to progress in their career or their personal life to consider these misperceptions and know how to effectively manage them. If unacknowledged, these misperceptions are so powerful that they can interfere with our beliefs and paralyse our process of (logical reasoning) thinking. In the end, they may lead us to either over- or under-estimate what we are able to achieve.

Out of the several hundred interviews I have completed over the years, the following key – and dangerous – misperceptions emerged.

Misperception 1: People Win Lotteries, So You Think You Can, Too!

This misperception is probably the most attractive one. The idea behind it is that we observe others hitting a "lucky" strike without any explainable reason – for example, your neighbour wins a lottery, a peer gets an undeserved promotion, or friends land amazing jobs that even surprise them. If such events happen to others around us, why shouldn't they happen to us? This legitimate question – "Why others and not me?" – is one that everyone asks. Widely internalising this thought, many people wait for their turn one day. After all, if others were lucky, why shouldn't I be one day?

Individuals need a strategy to avoid falling prey to this false idea. While luck may certainly come your way one day, there is no guarantee. To depend on such good fortune is ultimately damaging to your ability to develop your strengths and knowledge.

Our advice: Don't wait for your turn, as it will most likely never be your turn.

Misperception 2: You See Good Things Happening to Others, but Not to You

This misperception is the most "real." Others need not win lotteries around you, but it appears that lots of other good things happen to them. In your restricted viewpoint:

- Others get promoted and earn more than you, although you think you deserve it, too.
- Others have more opportunities from which to choose, thereby boosting their career progression.
- Others have more support for reasons that are not very clear to you or anyone else.
- Others perform poorly, yet still manage to move forward at whatever they attempt.

And to make matters worse, you don't seem to be alone in this observation. Other people around you also "see" the same things, making this misperception even more powerful. Without a strategy to avoid this negative mindset, you can easily become resentful and bitter, thereby adversely affecting your own life and that of those around you.

Our advice: Don't try to reason out obvious manipulation and self-interest. You will most likely never achieve favour by anyone in that type of environment. If things are not transparent in terms of who get valued or promoted, there is something fundamentally wrong in that organisation.

Misperception 3: People Get Away with Lying

You perceive that some people escape the consequences of lying, even though you are told to practise the opposite: tell and live the truth. The most important thing to recognise about lying is to understand why people do so in the first place. The simple answer is that people think they can get away with it! And do they? The "truthful" answer to that question is "absolutely," which is the main reason that people deceive others.

Lying is an amazing practical tool that is used as a shortcut to resolve any size problem. Its lifetime can be either very short (seconds) or as long as the truth is not discovered – which can, hypothetically, be eternity.

If you don't acknowledge this truth, the result can potentially be frustration. You can become upset with the world both within and around you, which may prove to be very destructive – for the most part, in fact, destructive to you. So, people need to acknowledge this reality and build strategies for dealing with such situations.

The main reason as to why people get stuck, frustrated, depressed, and resentful is that they are incapable of building strategies to deal with such situations. How can your boss or colleague clearly lie and get away with having whatever they want, while you choose to act with integrity and expect the same positive result – and fail to get it? It is almost an impossible expectation. However, that does not mean you should also lie to others to achieve what you desire. That choice is one you must make and pay for, either internally (by hiding yourself from the truth, while living in agony and soulless misery until you perish) or by being shamed and exposed externally in front of others one day.

Our advice: Don't stay in corrupt and harmful environments. The quicker you extricate yourself from such toxic situations, the less damage you will do to yourself by not mortgaging your unrealised future potential.

Misperception 4: You Perceive Failure as Pain

In your life or career, you attempt many things, but they don't work. Consequently, failure starts to feel like pain, which is a dangerous misperception. So many individuals refuse to be daring and try new approaches because they are afraid of failure (AKA, pain). Nobody wants to experience pain at any point, no matter the intensity.

Developing a strategy to understand failure and appreciate the lessons it may teach you is critical to going beyond that failure and achieving success. This approach is beneficial, whether dealing with personal or career decisions.

Our advice: If you are seeking genuine change, you must embrace failure, which will enable you to fine-tune your framework as you develop yourself or your career. Nobody has the miracle solution to success, fulfilment, or whatever you need to live a meaningful life. No single approach offers a silver bullet.

Change Misperception to Clarity

In light of these false observations and misunderstandings that challenge us on a daily basis, one needs to be able to think clearly and comprehend the risks in what we face. When you listen to others' stories of their lucky breaks, remember, they are just telling you a nice story, but not providing a practical framework that will set you on the path you need.

Everyone needs more substance than stories in life to develop oneself on a personal basis, as well as in a satisfying work life. Everyone needs a framework – a "how to" – to strategise.

CHAPTER 7

Why More Transparency in Management Practices Is Long Overdue, Inescapable, and Critical for Maximising Shareholder Value

This era may be the most exciting time for management practices – but only if leadership can truly commit to taking appropriate action. As technology transforms the way we live and work, we are closer and closer to reaching that goal we have been preaching about and striving toward for a long time. That goal is simply to bring more transparency in management practices in order to maximise returns for all key stakeholders – all – not only leadership and investment shareholders.

Technological advancement, not voluntary leadership, has indirectly driven this movement toward transparency. In addition, every field has witnessed three factors that have added to the momentum: the need to boost productivity, increase efficiency, and improve return on capital invested. As technology has pushed the boundaries of maximising business profitability, it has also transformed the rules of collaboration, competitive advantage through the democratisation of creativity, and the dynamics of sharing outcomes. Nevertheless, transparency is not yet fully here.

Resistance Is Unproductive

In spite of the driving forces, the need to become transparent in certain areas of management was inevitable, anyway. This movement represents the most significant evolution of all time for management practices. Although technology in time will continue to bring more openness and transparency in our lives, communities, societies, corporations, and nations, the unfortunate truth is that the result may not be something that everyone desires. Nevertheless, we need to empower transparency for ourselves and as members of society in order to make progress. If we are genuinely honest with ourselves and in our relationships, sharing the same or similar vision, we have the capacity to reach better outcomes at a more rapid pace.

In the end, transparency in management practices will serve all stakeholders. The more that such practices and policies become transparent, the better and more effectively they will serve their shareholders, customers, workforce, and even communities. Yet, despite this motivation, all stakeholders do not empower, or believe in, this movement. In fact, the opposite holds true in many organisations, with the result that non-transparency triggers huge hidden costs from wasted resources, finances, and time for all stakeholders – expenditures that many leadership teams might not be able to evaluate or recognise but that also limit the individual and organisational potential to outperform. Nevertheless, hidden or not, recognised or ignored, this cost is one that all of society continues to pay.

But it does not need to be this way. With genuine leadership, we can accelerate this transformation for the benefit of everyone involved.

A Practical Scenario Simplifies the Lesson

Consider this example. Let's say, you, as a manager, hired a person either from within the company or from an external source, sincerely believing that this person would perform well. However, it soon becomes obvious that you made a bad choice in hiring this individual. Initially, because you said "yes," it now becomes even more difficult to say "no" and to admit that you made a bad decision. Naturally, it is not easy for many people to accept that they made an error and – worse – by declaring that truth, potentially expose their faults and possibly place themselves personally at risk. Faced with this situation, the majority of people are likely to ignore the situation and hope that this bad choice will somehow disappear. But until, and unless, that happens, this mistake will continue to cause collateral damage in the organisation because you are afraid or uneasy about saying "no," even if it is to the detriment of company performance, just to save face.

But company performance is a very relative term that needs a contextual consideration. Although performance of 3% to 5% growth might be acceptable to many organisations today, it is inadequate when the leadership team expects the organisation, and the workforce, to outperform. When almost everything becomes mediocre in the work environment, it becomes very difficult to envision how outperformance would taste. Consequently, management does not even attempt to change. Why bother, since everyone appears to accept mediocre results?

But let's think for a moment about what you have just done with that bad choice.

By not being transparent first with yourself and then with your actions, you become the reason for a certain amount of unnecessary inefficiency, wasted resources, and unspoken collateral damage for your organisation. Eventually, your leadership team, colleagues, shareholders, suppliers, clients, and even the community will pick up the bill for that negative result. Although no one will actually hand you the bill, payment is unspoken, unrecorded, and invisible – and you are not held accountable for your irresponsible behaviour.

Nonaction Is No Longer an Acceptable Answer

In light of this situation facing many organisations, the big question is whether we should continue to allow this kind of non-transparency. Instead, should we be proactive and use all the tools and approaches in our possession to stop the bleeding away of time and money? Wouldn't that make sense? Of course, but before we attempt to change the world around us, it is important to take a deeper look into why the status quo has such power. Consider:

- Why do shareholders not demand that leadership implement change in order to gain a better return on their invested capital?

- Why is management unwilling to invest in tools and approaches that will bring more transparency into their practices, along with the potential for more rewards?

- Why do governments discourage more transparency as a rule in organisations by adding more bureaucracy through "check-boxes" for better resource allocation?

The answers to these questions can provide enlightenment and a faster road to progress. For one thing, changing the status quo requires energy and will power, which must be gathered, nurtured, and shared. It's far easier to let "sleeping dogs lie" and leave the responsibility to someone else.

But whether leaders, organisations, or governments continue to resist the movement, technology is accelerating the transformation to transparency in unprecedented ways. Change is inevitable and will eventually overcome resistance. The best action for employees and their leadership teams to take is to get on board now and prepare the organisation for that transformation.

Saying "no" to mediocre results, leadership, or individuals is a good first step for all stakeholders and offers the promise of better outcomes. Saying "no" to bad practices and policies cultivates transformation. Saying "no" to mediocracy in the organisations you invest in, lead, or work in, while focusing on how you can outperform, is the clearest route for positive outcomes in the long run.

CHAPTER 8

3 Principles of Making Organisational Change Not Only Happen but Also Succeed

There are many perspectives on organisational change. One size truly does not fit all. However, many leadership teams overlook the importance of some basic principles. Through our consulting engagements, we have come across the following three key principles that seem to be the most commonly overlooked when it comes to organisational change.

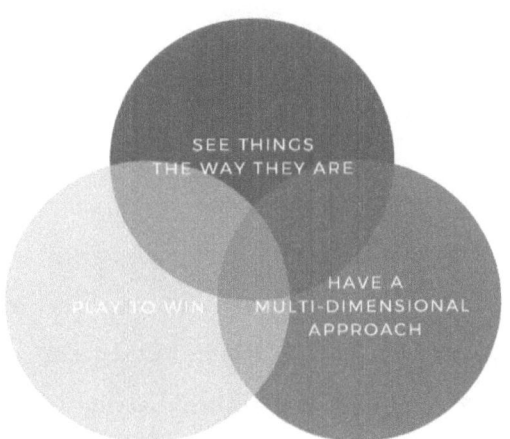

3 BASIC PRINCIPLES OF ORGANISATIONAL CHANGE

1. Having the Capacity to See Things the Way They Are

The number one reason why so many organisations fail to resolve their key organisational challenges is because they fail to identify the real challenges they face in the first place. In order to identify real challenges, you have to be able to see things the way they are – not as you think they should be – and that requires transparent management practices, courage, and true leadership. After all, it is only when we find the truth- that we can truly change things. Most organisations try to tackle the wrong challenges and, regardless of tremendous efforts, lasting change never happens.

2. Having a Multi-Dimensional Approach to Change

Have you ever wondered why top-tier schools select only top-tier candidates? It is simply because they want to develop top-tier graduates with the help of top-tier educators, educational environment, and infrastructure. They envision success through a multi-dimensional perspective. Your organisation can benefit from a similar approach.

For example, if you employ the best candidates and develop them with the help of the best leaders, management practices, and operational infrastructure, you will also achieve the best outcomes. That said, there is no point of employing top-tier candidates and then exposing them to "second- or third-tier leaders" and expect to get top-tier results. The outcome will be different. And if you are not sure if your organisation has such high-quality leaders in place, maybe it is time to assess that fact before you waste valuable corporate resources to hire, develop, and retain the most qualified people to grow your business.

3. Having the Audacity to Play "to Win" and Not Play "Not to Lose"

There is a significant difference between planning to outperform and simply performing. Almost all change initiatives start with a claim to make things better than before. However, majority of these claims lack the audacity to outperform, which means that you make changes to your organisation that allows it to play "to win" and not play "not to lose." In other words, if things were not going well before, then you have an opportunity to make things much better, not just a little bit better.

When you play "not to lose," your main concern focuses on defending what you already have rather than on winning. When you have an opportunity to change for the better, you should consider changing potentially anything. There should be no exceptions to this rule. Anything means anything.

Consider this scenario. You are a CEO of a company in which some units of your business are not doing very well. Consequently, you are eager to change things because you want those business units to perform much better in the future. Perhaps you can resize the units to gain efficiency, deleverage some product lines to refocus on key areas, pay more attention on sales and marketing, improve operational infrastructure, invest in the latest technology, or even buy new capabilities by acquiring other businesses. However, on the other hand, if you don't even consider reassessing the leadership team of those business units, you will not be open to change. When it comes to real change, you must consider changing anything that demands changing. Anything means anything.

Clarity, Openness, and Courage Make Things Happen

Caught up in resolving daily complex challenges in today's highly competitive market, leadership frequently lacks the time to view the overall picture of what is needed to outperform. But introspection is vital for the long-term success of the organisation.

Top talent, aligned with the company's mission, is a key factor. But top-tier talent alone is wasted without leadership's ability to see the situation clearly and determine what the mission should be. Accompanying such clarity is the willingness to be open-minded and consider the situation from all angles. And finally, when recognising what is necessary, have the courage – the audacity – to go forward and make whatever good faith efforts are necessary to outperform.

When leadership follows these principles, talented employees will be more willing to come on board and work together in partnership toward mutually beneficial goals. In essence, these principles can help management achieve optimal results.

SECTION 2:

HOW TO USE THESE TRAITS TO FIND THE RIGHT TALENT

The HR Perspective

CHAPTER 9

Let's Go More Human, Not Ape

"The data does not lie," goes the pronouncement, instilling hope in many of us for the development of new technology and the creation of more data to make things more credible and transparent. Hard data provides clarity and unveils previously unseen facts. It allows us to be more rational and foretelling in our decision making. Without technology and data, we would not be where we are today regarding advancements in many industries and management functions.

However, we should not single-mindedly believe that the creation and use of innovative technology and more data will also make "humans" more truthful. That being said, within each of us lies the potential for both good and bad – and no technology or data will change that reality. In fact, that potential is a very large part of what makes us human, and not mere apes. Although technology and data do make things more transparent and bring us closer to the ultimate truth, they do not necessarily provide the whole truth. At least for the time being, the ultimate truth still resides within each person, not in the machines or data they use.

In light of this consideration, the real and urgent questions for business leaders who are interested in sustainable business growth and management models should be twofold:

- How do we align business models and organisational environments/context that do not encourage people to be tempted or need to lie or manipulate others for their own interests – wherein the truth and transparency reign?
- How could we use this proactive approach to accelerate growth and developmental opportunities for all stakeholders: shareholders, management, employees, clients, suppliers, community, and so on?

If we are not able – or willing – to adjust our current management mentality and way of thinking as responsible and self-aware humans, neither technology nor data will ensure success or secure sustainable performance until we reach that ultimate truth moment that might potentially never come. After all, let's not forget, technology and data represent the utility, while humans are the source.

As B. F. Skinner once said in 1969: "The real problem is not whether machines think, but whether humans do." Our advice: Let's not lose focus on the human side of things – whether we are involved in work, family, or community.

CHAPTER 10

3 Questions for HR Managers to Ask Leaders

The transparency movement initiated by technology advancement will inevitably force many organisations to transform – not only the way they conceive strategies, but also how they hire, develop, and retain the right talent to grow sustainable businesses. Failing to recognise this organic transformation may result in catastrophic outcomes for all stakeholders.

To avoid disappointment in future expectations and drive their organisations to perform at optimal peak, every HR professional should ask their management team three simple, yet critical questions – with complete honesty on all sides – about the state of their organisational endeavours.

Question 1. Are We Really in the "Talent" Business?

Every management team should thoughtfully consider their response to the following query: Do we really need very talented employees to run our business and provide an acceptable return to our shareholders? Or can we get acceptable results with average talent?

Eroding your margins by hiring very talented people and then not using their talent, in essence, defies your shareholders (and other stakeholders). This strategy represents the most unspoken – yet easily correctable – misjudgment many management teams make.

Question 2. Are We Really in the "Brand" Business?

It is almost impossible to build a brand without developing your people. That said, if your management team is sufficiently serious and willing to accept the importance of having a brand, they should strongly focus on building their people first – or risk losing valuable talent.

Treating your workforce with the same importance and respect as the company brand allows a conceptual shift to something more stable, sustainable, and strategic. Employees, as a form of company brand, should reflect the business by being engaged, motivated, positive, committed, and personal leaders.

Question 3. Are We Crystal Clear on What Is Possible? Probable? And Most Likely to Happen?

Another critical mistake many management teams can easily overcome is overestimating what their people can "actually" achieve. They have hopes, wishes, and growth expectations for their people and organisations – without really attempting to know exactly the capabilities of the workforce on which they depend.

Management teams should be crystal clear about what their teams can possibly target, probably reach, and most likely achieve.

A Practical and Achievable Solution

Focusing on hiring, developing, and retaining only the right people within the strategic framework of what you are trying to achieve to further grow your business is a more sustainable approach. Management may invest in expensive recruitment, development, retention, and rewards programmes. But doing so is fruitless without a global strategic framework and only with the hope that things will turn out better some day in the future.

The practice of management today is no longer a "hoping" exercise. HR professionals have all the necessary technological tools and proven approaches at their fingertips to help their leadership teams make better and more reliable decisions about the future of their organisations.

CHAPTER 11

Why Is It So Important for HR Managers to Score, Too?

Many organisations consider sales employees to be their top scorers, the employees who drive the business forward. After all, sales growth, whether of products or services, is a key concern for all leaders – and it should be. Without sales growth, business would be nonexistent, and no organisation of any size would be able to survive and thrive for any length of time. Consequently, it is commonly accepted that the impact of the sales team on an organisation's success is critically important to its long-term viability.

HR professionals, on the other hand, are comparable to goal keepers in a football team. They are not generally expected to score a goal, even though, in rare cases, goal keepers may actually do so. But this perception is erroneous, as HR professionals are the ones who support the whole team and stand at the last line of defense as well as help discover, hire, develop, and support the right people, with the requisite skills that the company needs to score (succeed).

Although scoring is very critical for any given job, be it in support, operation, or sales roles, the key problem revolves around the agreed definition of what scoring means when it comes to HR.

Clarity Is Key to Scoring

Consider sales positions. Although it is becoming more and more complicated and complex, defining what scoring means for sales is, nevertheless, easier compared to other roles. What determines bonuses, promotions, and merit increases is clear, mutually accepted, and easily agreed upon in many organisations. For example, any positive or negative change in terms of agreed scores has a direct impact on a sales person's total rewards package, potential career growth, and even an employer's ability to retain that sales person.

With regard to HR positions, particularly HR managers, the definition is not as clear. Is it about the cost of running the HR function? Ratio of HR professionals to employees? The time to hire a new employee? Cost per hire? Engagement rating? Or other parameters that contribute successfully to the organisation's business growth? Leadership teams should make an unbridled effort to improve the scoring definition for HR roles so that these key employees earn a similar perceived value when it comes to scoring in their organisation.

Five Tips for Ensuring HR Team Players Can Score, Too

HR professionals need to be proactive, understand the vital part they play in the company's growth and success, and – at the same time – take control of their career. The following tips may be helpful in clarifying the situation and how they can score.

Tip 1. Never accept any HR role (actually, any role) without knowing how you are expected to score.

One of the biggest problems in HR is that not everyone is clear about how HR roles should actually score. There is no point in trying to do your best if not everyone above you, around you, and below you in the hierarchy clearly understands how you are going to score. Ultimately, you will find yourself in a situation where you spend more time trying to explain to others how well you are doing than actually trying to achieve anything! This scenario is a no-no. Don't do it.

Tip 2. Understand how others are going to help you to score.

If you naively believe that you are expected to score alone, you should accept that you are not in the right place or organisational culture to score. No one – no one individual – can win a game alone, manage a company alone, or grow a business alone. You should first determine how others – colleagues, line managers, leadership – are going to help you score. Only then can you make it crystal clear to others, as well, and get their confirmed understanding, agreement, and commitment on how they are going to help you to score.

This cooperative effort means that your performance parameters need to be linked to theirs, and theirs to yours, in a way that is clear and measurable. If not, forget about scoring. You will end up perceived as someone on the periphery, and perhaps just a nice person who seems to help others. As an HR manager, this place is absolutely not where you want to be or how you want to be perceived.

Tip 3. Focus on getting the right people to help you score as a team.

No football team has consistently won games based on a single player. Think about the most recent World Cup, where amazingly talented players could not save their teams alone, with the result that their teams were eliminated early in the tournament. So, don't think that you or anyone else alone will be the hero, outperform, and save your organisation year after year. Although a powerful and inspiring myth, it is far from the reality of today's business environment. However, getting or helping other leaders to find the right people to score is probably the most strategic thing you can do in your organisation. In turn, it will help you to score, too!

Tip 4. Stay relevant.

Even though this point is key, many people don't understand what it means. Staying relevant does not mean you should only be close to top management, hoping that others will perceive you as a top scorer (not to mention that not all top management teams are top scorers, either). It means that you make sure you remain, and are perceived as, a top scorer, even though you might change your team one day. Other employers or teams will still seek you out as a scorer, regardless of your context.

Tip 5. Practice, practice, practice.

This point may be self-evident. However, if you don't practice what you preach, you cannot expect to score as consistently as possible. You should focus on being out there practicing what you learn every day and what you want to improve to be better than today. Show others that you can contribute and help grow your business in ways that are creative, innovative, and sustainable. Let them see that you want to taste the same successes and be recognised for the scores you have achieved.

What It All Means

The bottom line is simple. People generally only remember and value the individuals who score, but not those who help others score. HR professionals need to score consistently so that they remain in the game. They also should ensure that others around them understand, agree, and accept how they score because what they do is fundamentally important and extremely relevant to the growth potential of the organisation. For HR to remain strategic, insightful, and be one of the key drivers of business, we need to bring more transparency around how HR – and, in effect, the entire organisation – actually scores.

HOW TO USE THESE TRAITS TO FIND THE RIGHT TALENT

The Hiring Process

CHAPTER 12

Tips for Hiring the Right People for the Leadership Role

Why is it still such a common practice to give leadership roles to people who are not ready for the position and accompanying responsibilities? With hindsight, in light of the eventual and inevitable failure of such individuals, many hiring managers often opt to repeat this error. But consider what happens when you give authority and accountability to someone who does not have a comprehensive understanding of what a leadership role actually means. It is very likely that the probability remains significantly high that the person will not be able to handle the authority and will eventually cause collateral damage to many people, to your productivity, and to your bottom line.

That said, there is a critical need for CEOs to understand the link between weak leadership and its true cost to all stakeholders – the management team, employee base, shareholders, clients, and customers. Part of the problem involves where corporations spend money – often, unfortunately, on HR programmes that do little or nothing to further the development of the individual employee. Without such forward movement, innovativeness and creativity stagnate, causing a drag on the quality and reliability of the company's growth potential. Another source of unwise spending is recruiting, hiring, and training employees who do not "fit" with the organisation's values or do not have the requisite talent – especially when it comes to the dilemmas presented by mergers and acquisitions, a clear situation where values and missions are likely to clash.

Truly Committed Leadership

Leaders appear at all levels of the organisation: senior staff, team leaders, unit supervisors, department heads, division heads, subsidiary presidents, and executives, right up to the CEO. To make the most use of valuable leadership talent, and ensure management succession and organisational continuity, consider the following pointers when you hire people for leadership roles.

Tip 1. Make sure that the employees who are given the leadership roles have an excellent track record of driving people behind them and not pushing people below them.

Nobody can be called a true leader if the person is solely using authority to make things happen – and not true leadership. Such circumstances typically occur in the military, not in the majority of modern organisations that face very different realities and operate under very different strategies. In a company, management should be able to track potential leaders' historical feedback – that is, input they might have received during their previous career roles through

360° reviews or other feedback tools that the organisation has implemented. The key point is the need to track feedback.

Tip 2. Create an "open mouth" rather than "open door" policy.

Such a policy allows people to freely provide feedback about the person in question at any time (before or after the individual takes on the leadership role). No leader – no matter the organisational level – should be immune to periodic peer, supervisor, and subordinate reviews.

Tip 3. If the employee is not ready or mature enough to grow as a person, it is senseless and wasteful to attempt to stretch their abilities.

A common conversation in such situations includes comments such as, "the person will grow into the role." Inevitably, except in circumstances where the individual exhibits exceptional commitment, the anticipated growth does not appear.

Tip 4. Emphasise the importance of leadership roles throughout the organisation on an on-going basis.

Create and deploy a communication plan that re-iterates the critical attributes of leadership roles. In addition, illustrate how these roles actually impact not only the person who is taking on the leadership role or the individual's department but also the entire organisational workforce. By indicating that every leader plays a role in supporting the efforts of other leaders, employees can readily grasp their own contributions to organisational performance and productivity.

Tip 5. Demand full accountability and commitment from the person who is accepting the leadership role.

If the individuals are unwilling to commit to performing their best, developing others, behaving according to organisation values, or show any signs of semi-commitment, make it absolutely clear that there will be consequences. Although "consequences" might mean different things to different people, leadership roles do not come with light compensation packages. If things go south and the individual fails to perform as expected, demand that the individual as well as the hiring manager take full responsibility – which should include a negative impact on both individuals' reward package. Tying performance to rewards, including the hiring manager, should be accepted practice.

Tip 6. Although it might be tempting, do not "turn the tables" and make things worse.

In other words, if a leader does not show commitment and fails to make an optimal effort, do not appoint that individual to another leadership role with a naïve expectation that the person might do better the next time. Unfortunately, people do not usually change easily. Management would do better to focus on hiring the right person to do a great job.

Tip 7. Spend more and quality time in selecting the appropriate people for leadership roles.

The company's money will be well spent in the long run. The golden rule on hiring to grow your business is simple: The more right people you hire, the fewer people you need to do a great job; the more wrong people you hire, the more people you need to do a job. The old saying is true: "You get what you pay for," and cheap labour comes with big costs! To stay at the cutting edge of productivity and provide higher returns to shareholders, spend more time seeking and hiring the right talent.

The Cost Is Avoidable

Consider this scenario: You appointed a person to a leadership role for which the individual is not ready. In addition, this person was never able to "grow into that role." Ultimately, after two or three years of the individual underperforming in the leadership role, you realised that it was a bad choice. Recognising the failure, you decided to transfer the person to another role, hoping for a better result. In light of the time and resources wasted, can you estimate the cost of this failure to the organisation? If not, you are probably not doing your job as a hiring leader properly either. Without knowing the hidden costs – in terms of recruiting, hiring, training, lost productivity, poor quality, impact of low motivation on other employees working with that leader, and so on – management cannot operate an outstanding and successful business.

The bottom line is simple: Leadership roles are critical for growing the business and outperforming industry peers in this extremely competitive market environment. By not spending enough quality time and, therefore, appointing the wrong people to these roles, you are defying all your stakeholders – shareholders, board members, management, employees, suppliers, clients and customers, and the community at large. Discovering, hiring, engaging, developing, and retaining only the true leaders to grow your business offers the road to success.

CHAPTER 13

What If Every Employee Had a Talent Agent?

Everyone knows that talented employees can make or break a business. But nurturing that talent is not so commonplace, though it should be standard practice.

The entertainment industry is familiar with the concept of a talent agent, the person who not only finds promising jobs for clients, but also defends, supports, and promotes their interests. Sometimes, the position responsibilities overlap with that of a client's manager, the person who oversees the client's daily business affairs. But beyond those tasks, the talent agent/manager advises and counsels the individual on professional matters, long-term plans, and personal decisions that may affect the person's career.

My son is a lawyer who specialises in intellectual property, with a focus on the media and entertainment industry. His passion for the sector, even without possessing the law degree, already positions him as a young authority in whatever aspect touches the industry. For example, without hesitation, he can tell you which movie was produced, directed, financed, and distributed by whom – not to mention naming the actors who have appeared in movies for at least the last 20 to 30 years, listing the movies that will be released in the next two years, and which ones are more likely to succeed.

On his recent visit home, our family got together to enjoy our favourite pastime – watching a good movie – which he obviously selected! Over the years, we had established an informal ongoing discussion about actors, singers, directors, distributors, and screen writers, speculating as to why some became very successful while others did not. In the end, we always concluded that the number one reason for failure or lacklustre results was simple: Agents did not guide these people well, perhaps choosing the wrong song to sing or play, the wrong role or screenplay to act in, or the wrong director with whom to partner. Consequently, as so often happens, even if a person is very talented, passionate, skilled, and knowledgeable, without expert guidance (and, of course, luck), the chance of success is low.

The Need for Talent Agents in the Business World

If this concept of talent agents was applied to the corporate arena, the impact would prove advantageous for both the employer and employee, as well as shareholders. The reality of the modern workplace is that the majority of employees navigate their careers without well-thought-out guidance or a plan individualised for their needs and desires. Although many organisations invest in "career development," the effort is mostly generic, with the needs of the company taking priority. Deadlines are pending, clients are demanding, and employees are overworked, leaving little time to conduct a true focus on the employee's performance (or, lack of it). Often, managers' needs are first and foremost, with managers relying on subordinate performance to reflect well on their own careers, pushing them further up the corporate ladder.

The role of manager, whether in a profit or non-profit environment, has eroded in recent years. Its original function implied that the person was responsible for taking care of people in the manager's department. In a way, a manager's job was to act like a talent agent for subordinates, ensuring that employees performed a role best-suited for their individual success, as well as that of the organisation to optimise performance. Today's managers are often too busy to "manage" the overall function of the individual employee and simply "oversee" what the employee produces, whether a product or service. To regain a genuine manager-employee relationship, organisations must focus on increasing value for all stakeholders – shareholders, leadership, employees, and the community at large.

So, the question ultimately becomes: If every employee had a talent agent, would it significantly increase shareholder value, as well as value for all stakeholders, enough so to make a difference? I believe so. In fact, I believe that this approach could significantly and positively affect all stakeholders.

The Cost of Ignoring the Possibilities

But, the naysayers are already asking, at what price do we implement such a concept? Critics would be quick to argue that an organisation, especially a large global entity, could not possibly assign every employee a personal agent. As a compromise, they are likely to propose doing so only for the leadership team or high-potential employees in the organisation – the individuals who "matter."

So, my first question to those people would be, "how much do you think it is costing you now when you don't do it?" In reality, the price is colossal, eating away the organisation's profit margins, slowly but surely. Yet, that cost does not appear in the company income statement or balance sheet, so no one seems to care (or acknowledge). Unfortunately, if the truth were uncovered, shareholders would certainly sit up and take notice because the leadership team is not optimising their investment.

Wasted resources, in terms of time and money, are the result of hiring and retaining inefficient, ineffective, and underperforming employees. Continual training of new hires to replace the failed employees is an expensive proposition in terms of potential lost money, lagging productivity, the risk of low-quality products and services, customer dissatisfaction, peer resentment, and overworked high-performing employees. Along with myriad other negative repercussions, the bottom line is unnecessary damage that chips away from the company results more and more as time goes on.

Paths to Success

For the talent agent approach to be successful, managers need to be creative. Positive results do not come only by throwing money/carrots at people, such as generous reward programmes or budgets for training programmes that sound encouraging but only offer a general effort to boost employees' know-how and skills. Whatever steps are undertaken to promote the concept would not require large financial investments to nudge the mind and thinking of managers.

Instead, the approach demands some form of collaborative creative thinking – perhaps expanding the scope and responsibilities of mentorship or coaching programmes, or actually including the term "act like an agent" in the position description of managers. By giving managers more responsibility and accountability – and leadership must emphasise accountability – to help others to succeed, and not just themselves, the entire workforce could rise to the occasion.

Managers would benefit by asking their subordinates two questions:

- What do you want to do?
- What do you do well?

The answers, when combined, should be able to point the employee's job duties in the right direction. It's simple common sense: By matching the individual employee with the task best-suited to that person's skills and know-how, everybody wins.

In fact, that process is what successful talent agents perform. They do not send actors to an orchestra's audition, or vice versa. The approach is not about simply getting the job done or achieving the company's goals. It's about getting the optimal job done with the focus on maximum value generation for all stakeholders while doing its best to meet the needs and desires of both the organisation and the individual. In the meantime, consumers and shareholders stand to gain as well, thereby boosting the organisation's long-term viability and performance sustainability.

CHAPER 14

Why We Need Talented People to Identify Talented People

If you want talented people in your organisation, make sure that you have talented people to recognise and select them. Of the many key strategies for success that leadership should employ is the need to focus on encouraging the most talented people in the company to help find and hire the most talented people. As Arthur Conan Doyle once said, "Mediocrity knows nothing higher than itself..." That said, there is no point in hoping that the organisation can get the results for which it is striving if it uses not-so-talented people to pick so-called talented people! They would not recognise the talent!

This issue is not about junior or senior hiring. Rather, it is a question of organisational culture and has more repercussions to the entire business of an organisation than just simply to the hiring process. It speaks to wasted time and resources (both human and financial), lost productivity, errors, and other negative results.

Misunderstanding Clouds the Issue

Many organisations, at the very best, arbitrarily define a select group of employees as their key talent – the producers, the up-and-coming leaders. However, the question is not who has talent. Everybody does! The real question to ask is how to unlock and leverage the talent in every employee, as well as the candidates who want to join the organisation. By doing so, the majority of the workforce will have the ability to power the business in whatever direction mandated by leadership. The ultimate aim of any organisation should be to hire and continue to engage the right talent who willingly aligns with its business goals.

Practical Steps Save Time and Resources

So, what can leadership do?

Step 1. Stop spending money on pushing and pulling people to do a job. This point is especially true when it is apparent that such individuals are not engaged, are underperforming, and drag down the unit's success.

Step 2. Start investing in tools and approaches to help identify, engage, and retain the right talent. Find such talent within or outside the organisation who can grow the company in the most efficient and productive manner possible. For example, if the company has implemented a referral system, ensure that employees do not simply refer "a friend" for an open position, but refer "a friend who has the skills and expertise the company needs."

Step 3. Continue to be selective when economic conditions result in a low supply of desired talent. Resist the urge to simply hire a body to fill a vacancy.

Step 4. Take the time to team build, engage in meaningful dialogue, listen to what employees are saying (especially what they are not saying), and train managers to "know" their staff. Most important, not only train the existing talented individuals to recognise the talent needed by the company, but also encourage them to reach their own potential through self-awareness tools and strategies.

The bottom line is simply this: Stop arbitrarily picking people and start knowing who can truly drive your business at all levels, organisation, division, function, group, and team if you want to truly outperform. Untap the hidden talent in your organisation and move forward, as an aligned team, to reach optimal results.

CHAPTER 15

Are You Betting on the Right People? 3 Tips for Leaders to Improve Their Chances

The essence of any successful business is all about knowing how to bet on the right people. Successful organisations depend on leaders who make the right bets on investments, businesses, markets, products, or technologies – and especially on people.

The following three tips illustrate how leaders can improve their chances of betting on the right people to grow their business and maximise returns for all stakeholders.

Tip 1. Don't Confuse Betting with Gambling.

For starters, one should not confuse betting with gambling, as there is a significant difference: Gambling is a matter of pure luck, while betting is a matter of strategy. Leaders cannot build and grow sustainable businesses based on pure luck.

Many people, unfortunately, do not understand this subtle difference between the two activities. In gambling, a person's skill set hardly plays any role in the process. However, betting requires the person to be deeply informed about the strengths and the influences of all possible factors that have the ability to affect the outcome of the process in question, either positively or negatively.

Without leveraging the latest approaches, technology, and critical data to hire, develop, and retain "only" the right people to grow a business, leaders take tremendous risks. In fact, without this knowledge and support, they are actually gambling, which can impact the performance of their organisations in the long run.

Tip 2. Only Remarkable People Can Create Remarkable Things.

Another important tip for leaders is to remember that nothing comes out of nothing. That is, if a company uses mediocre and/or archaic hiring approaches and tools, the result will only be mediocre hires, productivity, and outcomes. The ability to recognise and understand the type of people you hire, develop, and retain to operate and grow your business is mission critical to its future long-term success.

On the one hand, there is no point in placing mediocre people in roles where you expect them to significantly transform and grow your business. At the other extreme, placing a remarkable individual into a position where you only want consistent, acceptable, and stable growth is not an optimal use of talent either. Ultimately, you should only expect outstanding results from remarkable people to significantly outperform your competition.

What makes a leader remarkable?

- The ability to drive major transformational change and innovative initiatives and lead others – not with their assumed authority, but due to their convincing vision and highly compelling ideas and insights about the business.
- No fear of failure, accompanied by willingness to take highly complex, yet calculated, risks.
- Capacity to listen and the expertise to know to whom they should listen.
- Ability to move fast, with accurate information, and a focus on the best outcome for all stakeholders.

Tip 3. Only Talented People Can Identify Talented People.

If you want talented people in your organisation, make sure that you have talented people to recognise and select them. Of the many key strategies for success that leadership should employ is the need to focus on encouraging the most talented people in the company to help find and hire the most talented people. There is no point in hoping that the organisation can get the results for which it is striving if it uses not-so-talented people to pick so-called talented people! They would not recognise the talent!

The key issue involves unlocking and leveraging the talent in every employee, with the ultimate goal of employing the right individuals who are willing to align with the employer's business goals. By investing in tools and approaches to help identify, engage, and retain the right talent, both within and outside the organisation, the potential for growth in the most efficient and productive manner becomes closer to reality. In addition, by implementing a training programme that teaches employees to recognise other talent, the organisation can potentially reduce the cost of mis-hires, poor selection, lost productivity, and re-training.

Bet, Don't Gamble

Remember, you cannot build and grow sustainable businesses by making your bets based on pure luck and hoping for the best. That approach does not represent logical thinking. Leaders need to know better. They need to know how to discover and attract the right people to truly drive the business at all levels – organisation, division, function, group, and team – to truly outperform in the modern competitive marketplace.

To untap the hidden talent pools, both internally and externally, and move your organisation forward as an aligned team to achieve optimal results, it is imperative to start leveraging the latest approaches, technology, and data points. The sooner, the better for long-term success.

CHAPTER 16

Finding and Empowering the Untapped Employee Potential

Without the efforts of your employees, working in harmony with leadership, an organisation is not likely to achieve long-term success. If employees are not aligned with the company's strategy, they may be busily working while merely spinning their wheels. In fact, rather than truly contributing to the company's performance, they may be steering it down the wrong road.

Large organisations today spend tens of thousands of hours and tens of millions of dollars on activities that not only do not work, but also drive out top talent. What organisation can afford to waste such significant resources in terms of time, talent, opportunity, and money?

Leadership needs to create a clear direction for employees – encouraging their genuine engagement and providing structured guidance to willfully align with company strategy – with all parties striving toward mutually satisfying outcome. But how best to achieve this optimal state?

Defining the Hidden Treasure

Many organisations ignore, or perhaps they do not bother to explore, two huge sources of employee potential with the ability to boost the company's profitability and sustainable growth agenda:

Source 1. The "passively employed" population within their workforce (the forgotten talent).

Such individuals are employed, as defined by traditional means, but only perform just acceptable work within the organisation. Totally capable people, they possess their own convictions, passions, values, and meaning in life. But if the company does not use them to their fullest capacity, does not invest in them, and blocks their growth, then managers do not really explore these people and what they can offer. In fact, most leaders do not know how to extract the rich potential of these people in ways that could benefit all stakeholders. In effect, the "passively employed" are simply disengaged workers doing a satisfactory job.

Source 2. Employees who perform good, adequate work, but who are not identifiable "high-potentials" in tune with the company's strategic goals.

Acknowledged by their managers as being dependable, reliable, and effective employees, nevertheless, they do not share the vision (or, perhaps even truly acknowledge) where the company is heading and what it expects long-term in exchange for paying their salary. Managers typically breathe a sigh of relief to have such good employees in their unit. But such individuals, too, are simply disengaged workers doing a decent job.

By not encouraging these employees to do what they do best in the most effective and productive way, companies neglect the welfare of these promising individuals. An unfortunate comparison is to consider such individuals as a farm field lying unused, dusty, dry, useless, and lifeless. But if fertilised and nurtured, the field can produce ripe, healthy, and nutritious food products that will sustain others for years to come. The same concept applies to employees who merely do an adequate, maybe even excellent, job, but have nothing to show for it other than good ratings and monetary rewards.

To make a sincere effort to uncover the potential of these individuals, who hold so much possibility, managers need to ask them:

- Are you able to live by your values in our organisation and are you satisfied with your overall efforts?
- Does your job reflect your passion, desire, and need for meaningful purpose?
- Do you believe that your mission matches that of the organisation?
- Do you care?

By identifying the individuals in these two groups, and nurturing their growth, leadership stands an excellent chance of accelerating where it needs to go in terms of profitability, sustainability, community involvement, and public image.

Identifying and Refining the Hidden Treasure

In most organisations, naturally the leadership team is busy focusing on the overall company-wide picture and how it relates to the outside world, leaving managers to handle the day-to-day affairs of the business. Managers and supervisors shuffle mounds of administrative work, oversee employee activity, and solve daily problems, without having the quiet time to consider each individual subordinate and how that person fits into the overall organisational structure. At the bottom of the hierarchy, overworked employees complete their assigned tasks, with some more motivated than others.

With everyone concentrating on the demands of the workday, how can leadership and managers find the time to mine their employee resources and find the hidden gems – the untapped and productive employees who can help them truly move forward?

First and foremost, the leadership team must commit to caring for the welfare of all stakeholders and create a culture that will strive to align the majority of their workforce (ideally, all) with the company's short- and long-term goals. In addition, leadership must hold managers accountable for genuinely getting to know their subordinates: their pluses and minuses, skills and know-how, capabilities and utmost personal goals. But to support this extra effort, leadership must provide managers with the time and the tools to achieve this goal without overburdening them with administrative bureaucracy.

With leadership backing their efforts, managers might consider the following practical ideas to make a genuine effort to know their employees:

Idea 1. Treat each employee as a new hire. In other words, review the individual's résumé and credentials on an ongoing basis. Consider whether the person is under- or over-qualified for what the person does every day, as well as whether there are unused skills and interests that can be brought to bear on the job.

Idea 2. Conduct effective, efficient, practical, well-understood, and accepted performance appraisals. Employees typically cite problems with performance appraisals due to factors such as infrequent feedback, ambiguity, manager preconceptions, and so on.

Idea 3. Hold ongoing mentor discussions. Employees today want a mentor who can talk to them, on an ongoing basis, about what the employee is doing, how well the employee is doing, how the employee fits into the company strategy, and, ultimately, what the employee wants to do. Continuous and engaging one-on-one discussions can go a long way toward inviting confidences, boosting credibility, and ensuring that employees understand their contribution.

Idea 4. Conduct focus groups to discuss overall strategy and the direction in which the organisation is headed. Ask for employee input and ideas and take note of which employees are creative and engaged.

Idea 5. Provide employees and managers with voluntary self-assessment tools. Although not all people have the time or interest in finding out more about themselves, managers should encourage them to do so. The more a person achieves self-awareness, the more they are able to contribute positively to their lives, their work units, their employers, their families, and their communities.

Making the Right Choice

In today's modern competitive world, it is too risky for leadership to ignore these two significant under-used segments of the workforce. Managers should not lightly dismiss such wasted resources of time and money when small steps – costing little in the overall scheme of things – can boost an organisation's long-term success and standing in the public eye. The choice is simple: Surge forward, confident that the majority of the employee base is aligned with the corporate strategy, or shuffle along, reporting mediocre results through the efforts of a semi-engaged workforce.

CHAPTER 17

How Leaders Can Maximise Returns by Nurturing Undiscovered Talent

Everyone needs a strategy in whatever they do — or risk not progressing and waste time with unaligned efforts. In a world filled with unnecessary noise and involuntary misguidance, it has become extremely difficult to focus. Attention span is super limited, especially for the younger generations. Wishful thinking has become a pastime, and shortcuts are in fashion. Many people are tired of even trying and don't dare to dream (remain hopeful) anymore. These disheartening circumstances underlie why it is so important that leaders become role models and advocate true guidance, not stage deception.

The Key Issue

First of all, there is no miracle pill. Nothing comes from nothing. The only "nothing" we don't yet understand — from which this universe emerged — is what existed before the Big Bang. Rather than squander precious time on Big Bang theories (unless you derive satisfaction from it), leave such efforts to people who really enjoy thinking about them. Instead, we should focus on what we have the capacity and ability to create — how to shape, develop, and live our lives. But keep in mind, if you don't want to create anything meaningful, then nothing meaningful will result in your life.

Although the overwhelming majority of people are born with the capacity to shape, develop, and live their lives, only a minority have the chance to use a strategy or a framework to do so. Most believe this world is random, which appears to be, and wait for their turn, but miss a very important point: Chance is a question of movement, not standing still. This philosophy explains why so many people don't even bother to discover their real strengths and how they can improve them further to create something worthwhile.

Understanding the Pivotal Question

Actually, the real question is not about whether one is talented, passionate, self-aware, mission driven, well-networked, or action-oriented. The real question involves one's ability to compile these pieces together coherently, allowing the big picture to emerge in a way that drives real growth — not only for that individual but also for one's family, friends, work organisation, and community at large. It is also why so many talented, passionate, committed, or knowledgeable people remain undiscovered; they lack a framework or a strategy to create their own big picture.

In other words, we all need to understand that being "only" talented, passionate, or knowledgeable does not guarantee progress (or, as some prefer, "success" or "fulfillment"). If it did, then all professors would be "super successful/fulfilled" because they are super knowledgeable, all medical doctors would be "super fit" and live longer lives because they know perfectly how the human body works, and all artists would sell their artwork because they are just simply so talented.

Providing Leadership Support

As leaders, our aim should be to encourage, empower, and pave the way for others to understand the big picture for themselves as early as possible, because it is only when people view the overall perspective that they start believing in themselves.

As a leader, you want to hire, develop, and retain only employees who believe in themselves first in order to help your organisation thrive and outperform. There is a strong economic incentive for advocating that approach. It is not just "nice to have," but a "must have" approach to maximise returns for all stakeholders.

Consider this point: If people in your organisation wander around and struggle to do a fair job because they "have to be there" — that is, they need a job to feed their family or future plans, not because "they want to be there" — then they are exerting an average effort. Further, people in the "have to be there" group also have the potential to become barriers to growth for your business, because they may potentially lack the natural instinct and willingness to be creative and add more value than they receive regardless of anything else. If so, you are not maximising their efforts or aiming for ultimate efficiency in your organisation — which begs the questions:

- Why wouldn't you want to aim for ultimate efficiency if you want to maximise returns, which is the main reason why investors invest in a business and the right employees want to work for an organisation?

- Why would you want to leave money on the table knowing that there is actually quite a lot more left?

Discovering the Undiscovered to Maximise Returns

The bottom line is this: The foundations for an outperforming business include acknowledging the need for employees to learn how to act strategically, empowering them with personal accountability for their lives and careers, and providing leadership support not because it is "nice to do" but "must do" to maximise returns. With the appropriate and genuine support — in terms of expectations, rewards, dialogue, guidance, development, and new approaches — leadership can nurture a fully aligned talented workforce to become a well-honed, truly motivated resource that will drive future growth and innovation for decades to come.

CHAPTER 18

Why Leveraging the Generational Potential Works

When it comes to economic progress, both developed and emerging market economies possess tremendous opportunities to accelerate growth for a number of reasons. If businesses and governments start recognising these opportunities and invest accordingly, the potential for growth will likely be unprecedented.

Key dissimilarities define both economies, and they face challenges in different ways. At the same time, some of these challenges also represent opportunities. For example, in emerging markets:

- Individuals are generally more open to change, willing to attempt new approaches, and not afraid of taking risks because they are obliged to grow faster to catch up with the rest of the world.

- This characteristic, in return, forces individuals to be more creative and easily accept change because they recognise that the problems that they face can only be overcome by solutions that require innovative thinking and quicker adaptation to change. After all, they have been the champions of creativity, thanks to the continuous daily pressure for survival and a hunger to improve their current state.

On the other hand, in developed markets:

- Individuals face tremendous pressure to keep what they have "built." They are generally more risk-averse because they seek answers/solutions to maintain what they "have."
- While this characteristic also forces individuals to be more creative, it does not necessarily put them at ease with change. After all, they believe that the problems that they face should be overcome by incremental change and, consequently, do not see the need for drastic transformation.

The Extra Challenge for Emerging Economies

Putting aside these differences, the playing field becomes nearly equal. The proclaimed advantage of low-cost labour in emerging markets is an archaic thought; no nation will win that race because there is no winner in the long run. Cheap labour is generally unskilled and likely to focus on products and services that are mass produced. The quicker that emerging markets realise this fact, the sooner they will start to build economies that are much more sustainable over time. Price competition at a national level will only result, ultimately, in despair and deception, even though people experience an uptick in their overall income level in the short- to mid-term.

In addition, emerging markets face another dilemma. Investment in automation and robotisation of labour work have been high in emerging markets in recent years. Consider China's recent five-year plan, which promotes the usage of industrial automation, with robots and computer numerical controller machine tools identified as important areas for development – recognising that robots can help the manufacturing sector improve quality and efficiency, while reducing waste.

Coming years may witness a trend that is quite different and not so familiar in terms of labour force transformation in emerging markets. For example, consider these questions:

- What will happen to people who are under-educated, self-ignorant, and unskilled if automation and robotisation will not allow them to contribute as they have in emerging markets over the last 20 years?
- What will happen to those people who enjoyed an uptick in overall income by moving to large cities and working in low-level jobs, but now lack the same opportunity?

The key success factor for the upcoming transformation is investment in education, learning, and training – three very different things. Education relates to the state in many of the markets; learning relates to the individual; and training relates to corporations. The quality of these three key ingredients of success will solely depend on governments' ability to stay up-to-date, the individual's ability to be more self-aware, and corporations' ability to be, at last, "truthfully" socially responsible.

The question of which population or employee segment in which to invest in order to grow the economy or business requires a crystal-clear understanding. Without that comprehension, a misunderstanding of this question may not only lead many nations and corporations into the dark for decades, but also potentially become a huge bill we will all have to pay. For example, if by ignorance, a nation or business leadership fails to invest in upgrading the knowledge of the elderly population or a specific employee segment, the nation or corporation in question will most likely perish. It is crucial to emphasise the importance of this understanding across all our nations and corporations.

As life spans continue to lengthen, society has an obligation to retain people in the workforce to ensure more continuity of contribution. However, a longer period of contribution does not necessarily mean forcing people to stagnate in the same job or career for another 20 or 30 years. New approaches and technologies can empower people and keep them as productive citizens as long as possible, while maintaining their interest and desire to contribute.

Identifying Two Key Employee Segments

The younger generation has a role to play in moving both developed and emerging markets forward. However, millennials are not the only segment of the population that bears watching – and tapping.

Retired (or retiring) individuals often represent an unexploited resource in many markets, with few organisations viewing them as a potential source of growth and innovation. Unfortunately, the term "retirement" does not connote an immediately accessible productive resource, which presents a number of issues:

- A very valuable experienced pool of talent is untapped and remains idle until it perishes.
- Viewing something as a cost instead of an asset leads to decisions that are not necessarily value driven.
- Wisdom, a most valued virtue, is not shared and disseminated with the rest of the population as it should be. Consequently, younger generations continue to make avoidable mistakes, triggering further persistent costs to society at large.

Bridging the Generations

But the situation does not have to remain this way. We can create a brand-new, value-oriented employee generation by facilitating a process and deploying a technology to bridge the experience, knowledge, and wisdom of the retired population with a younger generation who possess authentic inclinations. That untapped value can prove simultaneously beneficial not only to individuals, but also communities, organisations, and nations.

The key opportunity for all markets is to rapidly recognise the potential in all segments of the working population and facilitate the empowerment process for every citizen. That is the only sustainable growth model that can prevail in the long term. With the help of technology and novel approaches, we could enable this process even at a national level, helping countries to accelerate growth in all markets.

HOW TO USE THESE TRAITS TO FIND THE RIGHT TALENT

Engagement and Retention

CHAPTER 19

Why Helping Your Employees to Learn More About Themselves is a Better Solution to Increase and Sustain True Engagement in Your Organisation

Self-aware employees + Clear company goals = Outperforming organisation

Many organisations waste so much money and resources on hiring, developing, retaining, and rewarding "the wrong people" – with little emphasis on overall employee experience and maximal use of talent. As it is important to recognise that employee experience can mean different things to different people, we have to be careful in using the term "employee experience/engagement." The focus should be on the issue of "employee vs. employer" alignment if our true intention is to significantly increase organisational performance.

Employee vs. employer alignment has two basic rules:

1. Ensure that employees are actually aligned with themselves (i.e., are self-aware).

2. With evidence of the first rule in hand, ensure that employees are willing to align with your company's goals.

If these rules are not validated within your organisation, you are wasting valuable resources on costly incentive programmes that might only bring incremental organisational improvement.

How Do You Know People Are Aligned With Themselves?

Obviously, personal alignment/self-awareness is not an easy task, prompting numerous perspectives, thoughts, and insights on the issue. Consequently, there are multiple ways that individuals can reach their destination. Although some will take longer than others, any effort is positive if it helps one to learn more about oneself. After all, a person who remains self-ignorant is not only a danger to that individual but also to society at large – a point that many people do not understand.

Of course, while we cannot expect every person to achieve self-awareness, anyone running a business should know whether the people who are working with them are self-aware. Otherwise, managers simply dwell in a land of wishful thinking, hoping that things will turn out well. In fact, they:

- Hire people and say, hopefully we made a good hire!
- Reward people and say, hopefully they will not leave!
- Train people and say, hopefully they have learned something!

- Promote people to leadership roles and say, hopefully they will lead!

You must do better than that when you run a business. You need to know if employees and colleagues know their strengths and weaknesses, have certain values, think about their future and actively plan for it, want to contribute, have a personal mission, are compassionate about others, and so on. You also should know whether those personal needs and interest are compatible with your company.

Employees and colleagues who have not thought about or are not even thinking about any of these factors are unlikely to contribute to the success of your company. Instead, they will be passive contributors who aim for the bare minimum. Regardless of whatever reward programme you deploy, you will not – and cannot – outperform in the marketplace with individuals who only make the bare minimum of effort. You will continue to waste value and resources for all stakeholders, including those passive contributors.

How Do You Align People vs. Your Company?

Conventional wisdom simply assumes that employees should follow employers' goals if they expect to earn rewards for whatever role they undertake. This wisdom also assumes that the source of the alignment should come from the employer.

In reality, it should come from both parties, as a one-dimensional effort does not work – or, at the very least, does not work well.

Consider: Would you like to be with people whom you know are indifferent to your presence? Would you enjoy forcing people to behave in a certain way solely due to the influence of your money and the rewards you can offer? These scenarios will not result in positive outcomes over the long-term and will not provide a foundation for outperformance.

What Can You Do Now?

The more that employees are aware of their capabilities and wants, and the more that they align with a company's business requirements (technical and cultural), such companies should outperform the competition. The issue is not whether people like the office environment or their boss, for example – the so-called "employee engagement/experience" per say. The right question to ask is whether employees "know" their capabilities and, thereafter, whether they "like" and "know" what they "want" to do in life. The accompanying question to ask is whether those capabilities and wants match organisational goals.

Sincerely, if you really love what you do and you have all it takes to achieve something, do you really care where you work? Think of those people engaged in start-up companies who are enthusiastic about what they do in spite of frequently working in miserable conditions, including garages, rundown offices, and the like. They possess creativity, passion, dedication, and ambition among many other things. Are they disengaged? Absolutely not.

As a first step toward moving your organisation on the road to alignment, obtain a data-driven assessment of what is actually happening in your organisation. Discover what percentage of your employees actually "know" what they "want to do" in life and are aligned with what your business wants to achieve. With a clear idea of the situation, think about how you can improve your current state. Start having internal conversations around these questions if you truly want to outperform. The alternative, if you are satisfied with the status quo, is to sit passively and wait for your turn the next time a self-ignorant person tells you what to do.

CHAPTER 20

5 Strategic Tips for Leaders to Truly Increase ROI in People

Whether or not corporate funds are abundant, leadership should always focus on the importance of optimal resource allocation in ways that will garner and sustain the most profitable results in terms of revenue, shareholder expectation, and employee growth. Throwing money at traditional HR systems and approaches that have been proven to fail or temporarily succeed until removed from the equation (e.g., short-sighted reward programmes) is not the answer to ensure sustainable alignment of employees with corporate strategies and goals.

That said, the answer lies elsewhere. A key ingredient of success for your leadership team is getting to know and understand the true needs and desires of your workforce. Possessing and using this knowledge appropriately, in conjunction with stating clear company goals, can prove beneficial to all stakeholders.

Yet, many leaders fail to understand the real needs of employees or often overlook their true intentions and desires. This lack, unfortunately, can lead to the long-term detriment of the organisation, countless unnecessary inefficiencies, and a significant risk to its viability and success going forward. To truly maximise returns on people, leaders should focus on investing time and effort in the following five areas to facilitate sustainable organisational growth and to outperform competition – while simultaneously engaging with, and motivating, their employees.

Tip 1. Invest in Transparent People Management Practices

Many organisations face a serious issue that involves the lack of transparency in people management practices with regard to calculating actual costs or, indeed, making little or no attempt to search for the true impact of nontransparent decisions. Such a lack of transparency triggers extensive hidden costs that typically take the form of wasted resources, financial expenditures, and lost time for all parties – from the employee to the leadership team to shareholders – thereby adversely impacting the organisation and its stakeholders. Hidden or not, these costs take a toll on all of us as we continue, over and over, to pay them.

The more transparent organisations become in their talent management practices, the more opportunities they have to outperform – and outperform well. Transparency is in the DNA of what is happening across many management domains today as leaders struggle with the issue. The only way we can make people management more transparent is by becoming more transparent in our decision-making process. In other words, business leaders need to be more open and honest in objective setting, performance reviews, career development, engagement, reward decisions, promotions, and so on. If we continue to keep these practices opaque and mysterious, we will never achieve any real progress in maximising returns on people. In effect, management fairytales will continue to prevail and remain a significant barrier in our efforts to improve organisational performance.

Tip 2. Focus on the Small Data (Common Sense) to Get the Big Picture

In a world where data is abundant, the best thing we can do is to learn how to find, choose, and use the information that is relevant to what we are trying to achieve. Relevant information should be unbiased, objective, and advantageous for all stakeholders. Although relevant information always stares us right in the face – in the form of "common sense" – perversely, we have an enormous ability to ignore it because of our self-interest. That recognition may explain why we have so many leaders "who know, but don't act." As Annette Simmons says in her book, The Story Factor:

"Facts are neutral until human beings add their own meaning to those facts… The meaning they add to facts depends on their current story. People stick with their story even when presented with facts that don't fit. They simply interpret or discount the facts to fit their story. This is why facts are not terribly useful in influencing others. People don't need new facts – they need a new story."

So, instead of spending an enormous amount of time and money to justify what you think is true with big data, you should instead focus on listening to the true and sincere stories your people tell you. These truths are less costly, more efficient, and amazingly reliable on the aggregate.

Tip 3. Build Trust Among Your People, and Don't Throw Their Trust Under the Bus

Trust is a very difficult currency to earn, and you typically own it once. Not many people know how to earn it or, perhaps, even what it entails. Not only does it take time to build trust among people, it is very easy to lose if you don't know how to invest it – especially when it comes to building trust with employees.

Beyond earning and keeping trust is another issue of significance – that is, the misuse of that hard-earned trust. If you share a good relationship with your employees, and then neglect and/or misuse their trust, it is almost impossible to regain it. Once you break the "trust contract," no matter what attempts you make afterwards to prove trustworthy, you will have to make an enormous effort and expend significant resources. And even with that endeavour, the attempt may fail. People are slow to trust again – understandably so – once they have been "burned" by so-called trusted individuals, particularly leadership. Understanding this point about human behaviour, managers should keep in mind that it is an essential trait of successful leadership to cultivate, earn, and retain employees' trust.

Tip 4. Don't Tolerate and Unknowingly Reward Self-Interest

Nothing good, so far, in the history of human kind, has emerged from serving the interests of only a few individuals rather than the common good. Your business is no exception and should be based on the interest of all stakeholders rather than the self-interest of a few. This approach is the only way to mobilise the efforts of all contributors to maximise returns for all. After all, if only a limited number of people benefit from organisational activity, the resulting impact on the majority of your workforce is likely to prove negative in terms of reduced motivation, poor morale, increased absenteeism, poor productivity, and more.

Tip 5. Focus on Getting "Only" the Right People to Do the Job

You cannot/should not attempt to change the behaviour of people as they rarely change. Hiring unqualified or mediocre talent who are unable to meet your expectations, even though significant resources are spent in training them toward alignment with your goals, is a strategy pointing straight at failure. Instead, focus on identifying, developing, and retaining only the right people with the right behaviour to grow your business in the right direction. The rest is just a waste of your and other people's time, effort, and money.

What It All Means

The bottom line is simple: We need common sense thinking to resolve the many organisational challenges we face. The critical factor is to remain in that "common-sense zone" and not lose sight of what is most important for the business – which, ultimately, is to maximise returns for all stakeholders. The foundation of every "business" revolves around this simple objective. If any stakeholder is not receiving a fair value, that stakeholder will always remain an obstacle to growth. Rather than creating barriers to grow your business, you need to do the opposite by liberating the pathway and eliminating the barriers.

The best remedy to maximise returns in business is to invest in management practices that engender transparency, mitigate self-interest, drive common-sense decision making, build trust among your people, and help you hire only the right talent to expand your business. Focus on these approaches or practices to outperform your competition. They represent a more cost-effective and reliable strategy in the long run.

CHAPTER 21

Why Losing "Us" Will Lead to "Me, Me, Me"

Many organisations have lost "us" — the team mentality —and unknowingly continue to incentivise "me, me, me" cultures. But it is only "us" — the employees who are willing to work together — who can thrive and grow your business, not only "me, me, me." Obviously, individual talent has a key role to play in a company's long-term success, but so long as the individuals perform in conjunction with the team effort.

Consequently, it is critical that leadership acknowledge this phenomenon and pay more attention to the kind of behaviour they are actually incentivising in their organisation. Too often, companies spend far too much effort and money on inappropriate and ineffective incentive programmes, ignoring the need for fresh, innovative, and "sustainable" approaches, which are long overdue.

Consider the following simple questions that can help your leadership team assess the situation in your organisation.

1. Does your current incentive programme encourage only individual or only team performance? Or both? If you pause to

answer this question, the remaining questions are meaningless, as you truly need a fair amount of reflection time to understand and assess why you cannot answer this question right away. If you can answer the question readily, then what is the rationale behind the incentive programme? Do all your employees clearly understand the programme? And does the programme achieve its objectives?

2. Do you factually know if the majority of your employees understand your business strategy? Do they contribute any input at all in defining your business strategy? If they don't, do you still link organisation performance with the employees' variable incentive scheme? Think carefully about this question and consider what actually happens. For example, what happens if the strategy goes wrong? Do employees ever question or challenge this policy? If they do, are you willing to listen to their concerns with an open mind? And if employees do not have any input into company strategy, why not?

3. Do you communicate your business strategy to the entire workforce or only to the management team? Do individual employees understand how their job fits into the company's — and the unit's — operation?

4. Do you allow leadership to be appraised by their subordinates? Do employees have a secure platform in which to express their concerns, contempt, or endorsement of their managers on a regular basis – say, quarterly? Or is it a top-down "one-way street"? In that case, no employees can provide constructive

feedback about their managers, but managers have permission to say positive and negative comments about their subordinates. As a result, what emerges is the risk of employees potentially providing artificial feedback about the state of the organisation, not only because they believe that is what is expected but also because they feel threatened if they tell the truth. This false testimony can go beyond leadership and reach the ears of the board members, key shareholders, and other investors at large who are not directly linked to the management team. In other words, no one can accurately and objectively articulate how deep is the river!

5. Do you objectively evaluate your managers on their ability to identify, engage, develop, retain, and empower their teams? If so, do you "actually" measure their progress and outcome on an ongoing basis (validating that this process is, in fact, happening across the whole organisation)? Or, do you simply let managers decide arbitrarily what talent to hire, develop, promote, and retain — thereby significantly increasing the risks blocking potential business, as well as people growth opportunities, by depending solely on the ability of a very small number of people without any systematic process and practice in place for validation and measurement?

In this age of super data flows and advanced technology, which allow us to make fact-based decisions as readily as playing a child's game at a fraction of what it used to cost, there should be no room for individual bias and manipulation. It is the collective power of a network of unbiased observation and assessment that should fuel the energy of your outperforming modern organisation.

Losing "us" — the true and authentic team mentality — to either the competition or to poor morale and unfulfilled talent is such a waste. To ensure long-term sustainable success, encourage both team and individual efforts, match efforts with appropriate incentives, involve employees in company goals, and, most importantly, create an environment in which employees feel safe to speak their minds — and hold everyone accountable at every level without any exceptions.

This perspective on work, available to anyone who dares to want only the best returns for all stakeholders, is the real future of work.

CHAPTER 22

Why Generating Value for All Stakeholders Makes Business Sense

The most productive, successful organisations ensure that all stakeholders (management, employees, shareholders, customers/clients) gain some form of value for their participation in the enterprise. Without a positive return – be it in job security, profits and revenues, productivity – the parties would turn their time, talents, and attention elsewhere.

What Each Stakeholder Wants

Each stakeholder in an enterprise has desires and needs that must be met for the organisation to move forward, to thrive, and to survive in the global marketplace. If the company is fortunate, those desires and needs overlap to an extent that encourages cooperation and shared effort toward achieving results. Consider:

- The leadership team wants the company to produce market results that earn a strong place among its competitors and peers. To reach this point, management expects employees to be innovative, highly productive, and efficient. By providing excellent products and/or services in the market, the company gains a positive public image, which, together, bring management their desired financial rewards, perquisites, and status.

- In return for their efforts and labor, employees want competitive compensation and benefits, work-life balance, feedback and communication, and an understanding of where they fit in the workings of the operation. Employees also want to know that their effort makes a difference, so that they can leave the job satisfied at the end of their work day. Security, both present and future, is also desirable to a reasonable extent.

- Shareholders spend money on corporate stock and expect a profitable return on that investment. They also want leadership teams who act with integrity, avoiding legal problems that could damage the company's standing in the community and adversely affect their investment returns. Shareholders also want communication from leadership on the state of the organisation's financial standing and future plans.

- Customers/clients want dependable, high-quality goods and services. They also require excellent customer service, with intelligent, knowledgeable, and trained employees having the authority to effectively address any problems or difficulties.

What Happens If They Do Not Get What They Want

If the different categories of stakeholders do not receive the value they legitimately expect, the consequences for the company's long-term viability may be grim. Typical scenarios, when the company fails to produce desired results, might include the following:

- Leadership may decide to cut back on resources, lay off nonessential employees, reduce or eliminate bonuses, freeze salaries, eliminate training programmes, curtail business travel, reduce research efforts, and take other actions that can eventually doom the company to stagnation.
- Employees are likely to lose their jobs; morale will drop; and employees will become disengaged and, potentially, careless, leading to poor product quality and lower profits.
- Shareholders will see stock value decline and capital gains drop, prompting them to sell their stock and invest elsewhere. In addition, they may express uncertainty and dissatisfaction about the company, thereby damaging the company's already spotty public image.
- Customers/clients, unhappy with poor quality and customer service, will take their business to the competition, reducing the enterprise's market share and revenues.

Some, all, or even more negative results can potentially occur, depending on a number of factors. If leadership is strong and willing to make an effort to engage employees in their shared dilemma, together, they may correct the company's downward spiral.

The Road to Value: Aligned Employees

That joint effort is the key to ensuring that all parties gain some form of value for their participation and investment in the company. Leadership must possess focused goals and a clear strategy first, before making the extra effort to get employees on their side. After all, having a straightforward goal, a generous budget, and skilled leadership may still not guarantee success without the support of the underlying force that drives the organisation: its workforce.

Employees, at least the majority of them, must align with leadership's desires, while ascertaining that their own needs are met. If the employee base is disengaged, if they feel unrecognised and neglected, and if they feel undervalued, they will not truly care what management wants. In fact, they may not even know what their work efforts are striving towards.

The road to that joint effort of successful cooperation begins with knowledge and information, regarding whether employees are a "fit" with the company's culture, as well as with their present occupation. Without that awareness, employees will come to work, perform a less-than-stellar job, and produce inferior results. But, possessing that knowledge, they will enter the office or factory or field site with motivation, energy, and the power to ensure that the company will generate value for all stakeholders.

CHAPTER 23

Keep Your Eye on the Ball! But Which Ball?

Throughout my career, I have been part of diverse global leaderships teams and held various positions of responsibility. Many years ago, one of our business leaders, who was responsible for the unit, frequently advised us to "keep our eyes on the ball!" During almost every monthly financial call, and at the end of every call, he repeated these words. "Don't forget to keep your eyes on the ball!" Nobody thought to question him about what he really meant.

At the time, my assignment involved building a new global product line that would be managed in multiple locations. My participation in helping to launch this business successfully was critical for my career; I had to prove that not only could I do it, but also that I could do it with sustainable results. All I had on hand to initiate the project was a very good brand and, of course, an approved strategic decision supported by the global leadership to invest in this new business. From my perspective, "keeping my eyes on the ball" simply meant that I had to ensure that the business generated revenues and profits within the established timelines – or, my position and reputation would be in jeopardy. Hearing our global business leader repeating his phrase, mostly on the financial calls, I assume, looking back, that we all implicitly thought he was referring to the financial metrics and results that he expected.

A Conversation and Good Advice

After a few other calls, I believed there had to be more to what he was saying. Knowing how critical the project was to my career and the company's bottom line, I had to be certain that I knew what he expected from me. So, I asked, "What do you really mean by 'keep your eyes on the ball'? Financial results?" To that, he replied, "Listen Ali, what do you think is the most important ingredient of a successful business?" My immediate response was, "revenue growth and profitability." To which he responded, "Wrong. Revenue and profitability are the causes of something else.

Considering the scale of our client base at the time, whatever we introduced in the market would enable us to sell a few new products to generate some revenue. With that in mind, I tried again: "Well, what about scale?" He replied in the negative, adding, "The people whom you select to work with is the most important ingredient of any successful and sustainable business. You need to keep your eyes on your people all the time. The moment you stop doing that, you will start losing." He also offered this advice:

- Keep an eye on the people you hire.
- Keep an eye on the people you trust to give accountability to lead.
- Keep an eye on the people you promote.

- Keep an eye on the people you select to fill critical positions.

- Keep an eye on the people who behave wrongly to others.

- Keep an eye on the people whom you develop and prepare to grow the business for the future.

And finally, "As long as you do these things, you will not have to worry about anything else. Trust me!"

The Right Focus

Being young and naïve at the time, his advice prompted a mind-shift for me. Ever since, the only thing I focus on in a business is on people. Plain and simple.

After a few years working together, we all moved on to new roles. While he held several CEO and management board roles in very successful companies, we kept in contact, as we enjoyed each other's company. And every time, I heard this phrase spoken in a business setting, I remembered him and thought about how so many people misunderstood this phrase.

Nearly 15 years later, I had the pleasure to spend another weekend with him, along with other former friends/colleagues. During one conversation, I said to him, "Remember how you told us to keep an eye on the ball? I did that throughout most of my career, and it helped me to achieve whatever I set up in my mind. But, unfortunately, I witnessed the opposite practice by many leaders. To use another analogy, they kept their eyes only on the cake, not on the people who were baking the cake. Those leaders were only interested in getting a piece of the cake. What do you think about that?"

He looked at me with great surprise and said, "I guess there will always be very hungry people on this planet who eat more than their share – and people do need to eat. But you know that very successful businesses are only built by people who engender trust with their clients as well as their own people. If you lose sight of this point, you are in trouble. Stick with building trust. And don't forget that 'people' means clients, your colleagues, and your employees. So, my friend, continue to keep your eyes on the ball – keep your eyes on the people!"

CONCLUSION:

Correlational Leadership and the End of Common Sense

Leadership is such an overused term that it has become an exclusive synonym for seniority or senior management, now struggling for meaning and respect in the corporate world. Today's organisations are so well-designed that they almost run on autopilot, with existing management systems and policies leaving almost no room for error. At the very least, these institutions are stable and immune to short-term deterioration without any remarkable effort because we have all come to value and appreciate regular and consistent results. In addition, compliance supervision and regulation make it difficult in typical situations for a modern organisation to mess it all up.

However, this scenario does not necessarily imply that the organisation is performing at the optimum level with efficient use of resources, both financial and human. In fact, regular and consistent results may simply point to just-acceptable performance. In any case, leadership continues to reap financial rewards, which may or may not be truly earned; after all, it has become very difficult to measure the true impact of any given leadership role. In the majority of cases, people believe that things happen because of their authoritative influence and decisions, not necessarily because of the other people around them. In light of this situation, it seems apparent that what is needed is an investigation into the true impact of a leader in isolation.

Checking the Facts

Decisions taken by leaders obviously have a significant impact on organisation results, for better or worse, but, can organisations directly link the results to such actions? So many companies go bust or perform at their lowest level because of bad decisions made by weak leaders – resulting in bad performance, unhappiness, dissatisfaction, wastefulness, inefficiency, untapped potential, poor customer service, no innovation, little motivation, and so on. One wonders if the average results of the many leaders do not actually link to specific cause and effect, but rather to correlations. In other words, the business community has created and accepted a new leadership definition that is purely based on correlation.

Logic and conventional wisdom are as follows: Company results are "acceptable," so I (the business leader) should belong to the "good leader club." But, in reality, no one has a clue whether those results were, in fact, caused by the leader or by the very well-established management systems already in place. If the result is due to the management systems and policies, then we are paying that leader a super-premium in terms of bonuses and other perquisites for something that was not worthwhile.

Unfortunately, many organisations do not measure this significant unknown factor, which automatically correlates company performance with leadership without validating the actual cause and effect. That said, a company could simply place any person with some intelligence into a leadership role for the same results. In other words, this conventional wisdom has led to correlation leadership – not causal – in many organisations.

The Road to Nowhere – or Success?

By not demanding the analysis of cause and effect in our organisations, we are traveling on a road that leads to the end of common sense and optimal performance. Consider:

- Shouldn't boards of trustees or directors hold leaders accountable for specific, measurable goals?
- If the results of a company cannot be linked to the actual decisions and strategies of a particular leader or team of leaders, where does the blame or praise truly belong?
- If boards (as representatives of shareholders) grant generous compensation and benefits to leaders who may or may not exert any influence on average results, what do we need to change that will allow us (as shareholders) to have the right to demand outperformance?

Correlational leadership can, sadly, only lead to encouragement of average performance and lack of motivation. When such thinking starts at the top, it soon trickles down through all levels of employees, who do not feel empowered to become their own leaders. Why should they bother, if adequate/average performance still nets rewards for their managers?

In the end, leadership – whether individual or organisational – demands responsibility, accountability, and the urge to do more, be more, and perform more. Personal accountability – cause and effect – is the driver that can return common sense to leadership.

REFERENCES

Dr. John McDougall, drmcdougall.com	Chapter 2
B.F. Skinner	Chapter 9
Arthur Conan Doyle	Chapter 14
Annette Simmons, The Story Factor	Chapter 20

INDEX